C

E U R O P

O

S

S

W B

B L I X A

S R

E G

A E

L

D

A

ITANY

Blixa Bargeld

EUROPE CROSSWISE
A LITANY

Blixa Bargeld

EUROPE CROSSWISE
A LITANY

Translation & Afterword
by Mark Kanak

Contra Mundum Press   New York · London · Melbourne

Library of Congress Cataloguing-in-Publication Data

Bargeld, Blixa, 1959–

[Europa Kreuzeweise. English.]

Europe Crosswise: A Litany / Blixa Bargeld; Translated from the German by Mark Kanak

—1st Contra Mundum Press Edition

140 pp., 5 × 8 in.

ISBN 9781940625560

   I. Bargeld, Blixa.
  II. Title.
 III. Kanak, Mark.
 IV. Translator & Afterword.

2022938827

EUROPE CROSSWISE
A LITANY

I've had a lot of tests done recently. The results have not been particularly good. My original plan was to travel to Paris, accept an award for my life's work, then on to Reims — see the Cathedral & then go on to Luxembourg, where the tour begins.

The latest results, however, are looking worse. At this point, "a biopsy," according to my doctor, "is absolutely necessary." Itinerary changes, anxiety — creeping fear. Antibiotics. Outpatient procedure. Waiting. Searches for alternative routes on Deutsche Bahn — Bahn.de. I find:

Berlin–Paris / Paris–Luxembourg

Berlin–Brussels / Brussels–Luxembourg.

A two-day internet search of the usual literature seeking justification for a culinary layover: *Michelin Guide* / *The Online Restaurant Guide* / *The New York Times*. — At least to eat well now. Further complications: My first layover falls on a Sunday, the day before the first concert in Luxembourg on Monday — not a good day for haute gastronomie.

The choices are limited, and the acceptable train connections further narrow the few remaining attractive options considerably. *Feinschmecker Magazine* rates "Waldhotel" & restaurant "5F," "Very Good," and it lies on the route to Luxembourg in Dreis, located not far from the Luxembourg border. I'll need a taxi, but that can be arranged.

ICE–Cologne.

IC Cologne–Wittenburg.

Pommerner Goldberg, Muedener Ley, Klottener Branneberg. The Riesling Trail. I haven't spoken with anyone all day; a woman on the train asks me politely if she can take a seat at my table, as she needs to plug in her laptop. The train attendant asks if the asparagus is OK (it was almost cold) and whether he can bring the check. That's the sum total of the day's discussions. In the taxi, on the contrary, I am barraged with questions: Are you on vacation? (Vacation? Here?) No, only a stopover on the way to Luxembourg. Can you earn good money in Luxembourg? (Haven't got a clue.) "The French were here in the past." What does he mean by "were here"?

"They left a few years ago." Aha! At least he doesn't mean Napoleon.

Nobody comes here for the fabulous hotel. Plaster statuettes around the garden pond. In the dining room: Gold framed, cream-colored figurines in nooks, electric candelabras, drapes, junk. Frescos: More junk. I don't know if the restaurant still has its three stars. The interior decoration, in any case, is definitely Michelin material.

I'm early, the first guest. A flute of champagne, a glass bottle of mineral water. The menu provides the usual suspects: Foie gras, caviar, truffles, lobster, fine fish, or in the language of the menu:

"*Parfait of Perigord-foie gras,*
Sole Goujonetttes,
Breast of Challens blood duck,
Cremeaux of Araguani Chocolate,
Passionfruit Cream Chiboust."

I consume a six-course pris fixe menu, which
neither lacks anything, but also hardly leaves me
smiling, and I take a glass of "Lagavulin 16 years" to
my room.

Dark wood. There's a snowstorm during the night.

The next morning finds the guests stranded in
the hotel. A tree has fallen further down the tracks.
It continues to snow.

They call me a taxi, & I am kindly driven to the tree.

I can walk from here, suit, light coat, small suitcase
on wheels, laptop, hard backpack.

Not just one tree has fallen. There are two,
there's another further on, where an old man is busy
removing the obstruction with an axe; he eyes me
suspiciously, as if I had taken a saw to the tree. If he
continues working by hand like this, it will be a while
before the guests can leave the hotel. Moreover, the
good man knows nothing about the second fallen tree.
Nobody knows. I am the first to traverse this impass-
able no man's land. I halt at the end of the road and
hope that the taxi isn't stopped by further catastrophes,
that the driver can even find me, that my batteries will
last long enough in case I have to call the hotel. I wait.
It arrives.

IC 438: Wittlich HBF, Trier HBF, Igel (GR), Wasserbillig, Luxembourg.

The train is empty. I have a compartment to myself, where I can memorize the text:

Ich warte mit geschlossenen Augen
   I'm waiting with closed eyes
warte auf den Morgen
   waiting for the morning
ich warte auf die Putzkraft
   I'm waiting for the cleaner
die soll den Blumenmüll entsorgen
   to dispose of the flower waste

Ich warte auf die Kellnerin
   I'm waiting for the waitress
hab Monde mir bestellt…
   moons are what I've ordered…
Ich warte durch die ganze Zeitung
   I'm waiting throughout the newspaper
bis es Zeit ist für die Welt
   until it's time for the world

Ich warte mit dem Kugelschreiber
   I'm waiting with the ballpoint pen
Auf den Einfall der Ideen
   for ideas to strike
Ich warte warte warte weiter
   I'm waiting waiting waiting

Bis es Zeit ist zurückzugehen
until it's time to return

Ich warte in den Zwischenräumen
I'm waiting in the gaps in between
Vorgeblich ungeschützt
allegedly unprotected
Ich warte auf die neue Sprache
I'm waiting for the new language
Die die mir dann nützt
that that will be of use to me

Ich warte auf die Dopamine
I'm waiting for the dopamines
Die innerlich versprochen sind
that have been internally promised
Ich warte auf die Vorstellung
I'm waiting for the vision
dass der Film endlich beginnt
that the film finally begins

Ich warte vor dem Automaten
I'm waiting at the machine
Warte auf mein Geld
waiting for my money
Ich warte, bis ein Stückchen Weltraumschrott
I'm waiting until a lump of cosmic junk
Direkt vor meine Füße fällt
crashes down at my feet

Ich warte taste schwarze Tasten
I'm waiting touching black keys
weil Weiss bisher nur irrt
because white as yet is wrong
Ich warte warte warte weiter warte unbeirrt
I'm waiting waiting further waiting waiting unperturbed

Ich warte auf Katzengangeslärm
I'm waiting for the cat's gait's racket
Ich warte auf Fischessang
I'm waiting for the fishes' song
Ich warte auf den einen großen
I'm waiting for the single big
unbeherrschten Klang
irrepressible gong

Ich warte auf die dunklen Massen
I'm waiting for the dark masses
zwischen den Sternen noch unentdeckt
between the stars still undiscovered
Ich warte auf die Untertassen
I'm waiting for the saucers
von den Nazis in den Anden versteckt
kept in the Andes by the Nazis under cover

Ich warte am Rand der Welt
I'm waiting at the edge of the world
an dem es selbst Atomen schwindelt
where even atoms feel giddy

Ich warte direkt am schwarzen Loch
  I'm waiting right by the black hole
Ich warte warte immer noch
  I'm waiting waiting still waiting
Ich warte unverdrossen
  I'm waiting undeterred
Ich warte auf meiner Eisbergspitze
  I'm waiting for my iceberg tip
am Ende der Physik
  at the end of all physics
auf Novemberhitze
  for November heat
und auf Dinge, die's nicht gibt
  and for things that don't exist
ich warte warte immer weiter
  I'm waiting waiting incessantly
letztendlich auf Musik
  ultimately for music

My doctor calls from Berlin, he considers it important to inform me at once. The results are in. I am initially relieved: No all clear, but postponement. The planned procedure: We'll do it all again in half a year, then we'll decide what to do. The concerts can take place as planned.

Ich warte auf die eine
  I'm waiting for the one

8

die ihren Namen wohl verdient
    that well deserves its name
immer da war immer recht hat
    always been there always right
auf die eine die die Sonne ausgräbt
    for the one who digs out the sun
das Gesetz der Gräber aufhebt
    that abolishes the law of the graves
Ich warte auf die die taktlos erntet
    I'm waiting for the one who harvests tactlessly
honigtriefend
    honey dripping
barfuß tanzend ohne Hemmschuh
    dancing barefoot without shoe
die Ton für Ton der Starre entkommt
    who escapes tone by tone from rigidity
die jedem auf Anhieb bekannt vorkommt
    who seems familiar to everyone at once
Ich warte bis sie Türen Tore Schleusen öffnet
    I'm waiting until she opens doors, gates, sluices
bis sie wolkenbrechend — Weckruf Fanfare —
    until she breaks the clouds — wake-up call fanfare —
überraschend aus dem Hinterhalt sich stürzt
    surprisingly rushes out of the ambush
Ich hoffe sie zettelt eine Hymne an
    I hope she starts a hymn
Ich warte bis es nichts mehr zu warten gibt
    I'm waiting until there's nothing left to wait for

das leben ist kein Irrtum, kein Irrtum und Musik
  life is no mistake, no mistake and music
Ich warte
  I'm waiting
Ich warte immer noch
  I'm waiting still

Luxembourg. How to spend the rest of the day?
The Musée National d'Histoire et d'art has an exhibition on entitled: The Greeks & the Sea. Subtitle: Fish
platters of antiquity from the collection of Florence
Gottet. — Terrific, I like this kind of exhibition. I
travel through the same cities again and again, the
European capitals, the metropoli of the Western World
plus Tokyo, Shanghai, and Beijing. Occasionally this
city or that off the usual route. One advantage my
job provides as a traveling musician. Museums and
Art collections over and over. Visits with old friends:
The great lightening tube in Dresden (ein Fulgurit),
Albrecht Dürer's: *The Martyrdom of Ten Thousand
Christians* in Vienna, or Canova's *Napoleon* in the court
of the "Palazzo di Brera" in Milan — Napoleon as God.
I have developed favorites. There are many rooms in
my personal, global chamber of wonders, which I seek
out for education & entertainment, but even a small
temporary exhibition like this one: Fish platters of
the antiquity from the collection of Florence Gottet.
*The Greek platters of the Florence Gottet collection form the
core of the special exhibit created in cooperation with the*

National Museum for Antiquities. Prepared marine specimens and fossils from the Berlin Museum of Natural History enrich the Exhibit: The fish platter, frequently included in tombs (used as Grabbeigaben), are noteworthy for their decoration as well as standing for the synthesis of life and death. (Something in the last sentence doesn't make sense). *The symbolism of the fished portrayal only becomes clear in the context of burial. The images of marine creatures are revealed simultaneously as a message of consolation, to annunciation of Life after Death, the enameled fish thus become a metaphor.*

Just what the doctor ordered, a manageable exhibit of existential scope in the form of fish platters. Precisely what I need. A manageable exhibit of existential scope in the form of fish platters. Before lunch.

Lunch: Apoteka.

If you can believe *Michelin*, the chef, a former student of Paul Bocouse, looks like Robert Smith of "The Cure," and his kitchen — he calls it "Kitchen Rock" — is *"fun and fusion, trendy and colorful, playing with colors and textures and even using a few decorative accessories. From South America to Japan via the Himalayas, our young prodigy draws inspiration from all over the world. Morels and Pineapple, calf liver and onion chutney, red mullet and coconut, crayfish and Bounty Bar...."*

Bounty Bar?

I go there anyway and: I am the only guest.

The menu's a bit confusing:

WALT DISNEY SESSION
SOURIS D'AGNEAU A LA PECHE KETCHUP SPÄTZLE
SAUTÉS SOLARIUM

I choose

SIMPLE LIFE EXPENSIVE
AL DENTE DI TAGLIATELLE SUR TRUFFE
ROQUETTE
PARMESAN GRAND PERE

Tagliatelle with truffles. What can go wrong with
that? — And a dessert.

100% RODEO CHOCO
DEFILE CHOCO RABANE EN 10 FACONS

The Chocolate Sensation arrives without a Bounty,
but with M 'n' M 's and every possible other bauble,
served in an enormous glass goblet.

The rest of my desserts are as follows:

A man fucking a rubble heap. That's it. Clear.
There's nothing more to say.

A piece of mango still dangles in the horizon,
meaningless. Back to the hotel. Siesta. Email.
Television.

Evening: Restaurant Claire Fontaine: Politicians,
Loud Americans, Russians in suspenders … The usual
crowd for a restaurant with stars. Good service —
Good night.

Rockhall, 5 Avenue du Rock 'n' Roll, Esch zur Alzette, Luxembourg.

Die Wellen

Nagorny Karabach

Dead Friends

Ich hatte ein Wort

Youme & Meyou

Sabrina

Let's Do it a Da Da

Weil Weil Weil

Unvollständigkeit

Tagelang Weiss

Von wegen

Die Befindlichkeit des Landes

Susej

Ich warte

The tour bus is a double-decker; the upper deck has sixteen sleeping compartments all told — twelve with a lounge up front, four more in a small section behind the stairs, and another "lounge," that is corner bench, television, DVD and CD player, stereo, etc.

There are no beds below, just chairs and tables, a tea kitchen: microwave, refrigerator, and more audio-visual entertainment.

The bus is equipped with a satellite connection through a German provider. The lease agreement contracted to a German firm provides internet access throughout the bus (WiFi!) with no additional fees, as long as we are in Germany. Access outside Germany is charged according to download bandwidth used.

The last band that traveled with our driver apparently failed to understand the terms; perhaps they weren't very good in geography, as least as far as Europe is concerned. I think it was Korn, but I'm not certain. They downloaded movies and were surprised when they got a bill for €6,000 at the end of the trip. The "crew" also has a bus like this one but usually travels by night — that is, the bus serves as their hotel. (Our transportation arrangements are quite a bit better than they were in the days when the band plus the sound technician plus the driver plus instruments plus tour leader all traveled in a nine seat Mercedes bus (with an expandable roof, beds on top). There was no need for another vehicle. There were no "roadies." We took care of the setting up and breaking down ourselves …)

The band chose their bunks first as they always did, each according to his preferences. When I arrived — I traveled from Luxembourg by train — all the seats were marked off with gaffer tape. I had been considerately consigned to the rear lounge according to my desire. After every concert, drinks, ice cubes, and anything edible and portable left over backstage are loaded onto the bus. Each band lists different demands in their contract. Our rider is surely among the most absurd: rice milk, soy milk, organically farmed fresh fruit and vegetables, a citrus juicer and an electric juice extractor, a bottle of "Dom Perignon" champagne, Russian vodka — no, "Gorbatschow" is not Russian vodka —, English gin, red and white wine from specified vineyards & of particular provenance; beer, juice, water, etc. (Defined in a codicil to the contract: 22 pages.) There are six vegetarians on the tour, no religious restrictions, only a few allergies. We ate whatever was left behind by the previous band, their remaining ton of potato chips, however, were disposed of at the next rest stop. The windows of the bus are mirrored on the outside. It's a little dark inside. With all available light sources (whose color can be specified and which can blink and pulse, as well) it's still too dark to read. On learning this, we immediately complained to the bus company. They were somewhat surprised; nobody had ever ordered a reading lamp. The interior design is more geared for entertainment — a surround sound system, luxury wood installations, mirrored surfaces; better than American tour buses, which generally look the way Americans imagine European (19th century) luxury. Most, furthermore, hand-framed Christian aphorisms around the bus: *"Lord, you said that once I decided to follow you, you would walk with me all the way. But I notice that during the most troublesome times in my life, there is only one set of footprints. I don't understand why you left my side when I needed you most." The Lord said: "My precious child, I never left you during your time of trial. Where you see only one set of footprints, I was carrying you."*

The text is set against a background of footprints, blue sky and sand dunes. My, my, my …

Luxembourg → Milan, Christoph Luxenberg: The Syro-Aramaic reading of the Koran: A contribution to the decoding of the language of the Koran.

We take a break in Alsace. We haven't stopped at Autobahn rest stops for a long time. The bus has internet access, and seeking acceptable restaurants breaks the monotony. "Google Maps" is synchronized with the bus's navigation system. Where will we be between 1:00 and 2:00 PM? Search the surrounding area: Restaurant. "Auberge du Cerf" in Illkirch Grafenständen, "L'Auberge du Ried" in Erstein or "Hotel-Restaurant Ramstein" in Scherwiller? — Nah... not really necessary. After reviewing the menu on the internet: "Zum Schnogaloch" in Obernai. Telephone reservation for nine. ("German? French? English?"). Obernai: Wood beam buildings, flower boxes in the windows. Schnakenloch is on the Sternenplatz, in a little street behind the carousel. What follows is the invasion of an idyllic village inn by a civilized rock band. "Flammenkuchen" is only available in the evening. Salad with goat cheese, sauerkraut tort, trout with almonds, kidneys in cognac, beer. Wine. The driver doesn't mind the detour: "As long as you don't keep demanding to be driven to this chalet or that to visit your rich friends like Lenny Kravitz..." The tour manager buys an electric juicer in a nice little village appliance shop. The juicers that the bus companies provide are usually not the real thing.

It might look as if eating and drinking are my only activities. What else can I do? I rely on lunch. We're on in the evening program, & we go on last, late; if there are opening acts: even later. After that most cities close down the sidewalks. The restaurants have long since closed. Catering for the band & crew is mostly afternoons, after the soundcheck; I cannot & will not eat so late before going on stage. After the show my only option is hotel room service: I forego it — usually. Chocolate bars from the minibar. Milan is a fashion city, there is really nothing for me there, except — and this counts for all of Italy — shoes. I could also say: I buy my shoes in Italy. I used to only own one pair of shoes; when they fell apart & couldn't be worn, even with duct tape, I bought a new pair. There was the black rubber boot period. There was a cowboy boots period. I have been in the Italian shoe period for a long time now — shoes with laces. Shoes that look like the idea of a shoe, platonically speaking.

I now own more than one pair of shoes. I was in a shoe shop in Bologna when Ratzinger was proclaimed Pope; the staff was glued to the radio, I was trying on shoes. I sat in a wheelchair in Sicily — a respectable sized splinter had been removed from my foot — and bought shoes in the Old Town of Catania; I only wore the left one for a while. Drizzling rain.

I've bought shoes next to the Cathedral in Milan more than once. Moreschi is closed today. No shoes. Lunch.

"Cracco Peck" is now called simply "Cracco." Cracco separated from Peck. I am guided to an elevator and transported down two floors, 10 meters below ground. High ceilings and sound absorbing walls. Interior

designers rarely take the trouble to consider the
acoustics of a room. No music. The waiters are better
dressed than I am. As a single diner I am seated at a
round table next to a column, a side table for vagrant
gastrographs; a Korean "food blogger" is seated at a
similar table across from me. With the *Michelin Guide*
open on the table in front of him. He photographs
every single course. The waiters have to wait with the
sauces several times, so that he can shoot before and
after photos. I order the same "menu" and photograph
nothing. Good that Cracco and Peck split up — the
meal is superb. "*Spaghetti ricci di mare e caffe*, Spaghetti
with sea urchin and coffee." But they won't give me a
souvenir menu. (But the Korean gets one.) They give
me a Rubik's Cube instead. Why? If I'd only taken
pictures or at least taken notes, the service would
have been more attentive.

"Alcatraz": I've been here often:
Die Wellen
Nagorny Karabach
Dead Friends
Let's Do it a Da Da
Weil Weil Weil
Unvollständigkeit
Tagelang Weiss
Rampe / Von wegen
Befindlichkeit
Susej
Ich warte

We travel overnight. Rocked in our berths, shaken in sleep depending on the road conditions, to Naples. 800 km. Arrive broken. The hotel is right on the water, on the Gulf of Naples, in Santa Lucia. Fortunately, my room is ready.

A few hours until rehearsal. Shoe shopping? Pompeii. I inquire about a car & driver at the reception. Wait for the return call, which never comes, & finally give up. There's not really enough time for Pompeii. I was in Naples two weeks ago, fleeing a female stalker who was besieging my building in Berlin. I like Naples. "Nea Polis," the new city, which was originally a Greek settlement. Giordano Bruno came from here, lived here, studied here, for decades, before they burned him at Campo di Fiore in Rome. Naples was one of the largest cities in the world then, following Constantinople, Cairo, Tabrez, and Paris. Certainly the most densely populated: 250,000 inhabitants within the city walls, since building outside the walls was prohibited under Spanish rule. I look for a market in the old town, for my old hotel, to orient myself in my memory. I find nothing. No shoes, either. Pranzo: "Vecchia Cantina," modest. *Bruschette misti, Alice marinate, Spaghetti ai Polpi, Dolce, Espresso.* I only drink coffee here. Only in Italy.

Teatro Mediterraneo. A fascist cube with a monumental pillared façade, marble, frescoes, nothing politically offensive. It was renovated in the fifties. Very imposing. The seats in the great theater are exceptionally roomy and comfortable, almost like TV chairs.

Intro / Die Wellen
Nagorny Karabach
Dead Friends
Let's Do it a Da Da
Weil Weil Weil
Unvollständigkeit
Tagelang Weiss
Rampe / Von wegen
Sabrina
Die Befindlichkeit des Landes
Susej
Ich warte

Pizza in the dressing room.

Naples → Bologna, a break half way into Umbria. We have to take an elevator up to the old town, Todi is situated on a mountain. A very old city, supposedly built by Hercules. Ristorante "Pane e Vino." After lunch (among other things a wonderful salad of little, raw artichokes) we stock up on local specialties, olive oil & wine. Souvenirs.

The bus has ample storage space. We doze until Bologna.

"Estragon," Via Stalingrado 83, Parco Nord, industrial area.

Intro / Die Wellen
Nagorny Karabach
Dead Friends

Let's Do it a Da Da
Weil Weil Weil
Unvollständigkeit
Tagelang Weiss
Rampe / Von wegen
Sabrina
Die Befindlichkeit des Landes
Susej
Ich warte
Sushi delivery after the show. My room is just
large enough for me and my suitcase. Attempt to sleep
in a stationary hotel bed. At night someone outside
starts their motorcycle — or so I think — again and
again. I open the window early the next morning: An
agricultural exhibition has been set up outside on
the Piazza. Tractors arranged according to size and
manufacturer, side by side in rows. Lindner, Claas,
and Lamborghini. Huerlimann, McCromick. Special
machines, equipment.

Lunch with Enrico Croce, the Italian producer/
organizer responsible for the Italian leg of our trip.
Bologna is his hometown. Italy was always good to us.
We are German. We ♥ Italy. We have the day free.

Free, that means traveling.

After Lunch: Bologna → Graz.

"Welcome to the augarten art & design hotel!
Our design/boutique hotel is simultaneously a gallery —
with artworks from over 140 famous artists. Enjoy your stay,

business or personal, the art in an extraordinary ambiance as well as service and comfort adapted to your requirements. We will indulge you with a maximum of individual liberty.

Indoor swimming pool, fitness room, solarium, sauna and hotel bar are open around the clock and also our breakfast times are flexible. Early check in and late check out is certainly possible on request.

Adjacent to the hotel you will find the restaurant Magnolia — certified by Gault Millau. Not only do our guests love it, but it's also very popular with the locals. Offering not only room service and catering for meetings, Herbert Schmidhofer and his team will fulfill all your culinary desires.

Open: Mo–Fri, reservations requested."

It is Sunday. Nothing's open, and it's raining. I order a gin and tonic at the bar, which is served by the receptionist, and have a look at the pictures on the walls: Valie Export, Günter Brus, Kippenberger, A.R. Penck, etc. The bartender orders me a pizza from a local delivery service. I retire to my designer room and dive into the internet.

The Korean food blogger has uploaded his photos from "Cracco": http://blog.empas.com/elenic/read. html?a=9684175

I use Google to translate the page from Korean. He boldly maintains that he was the sole, solitary diner there, which simply isn't true. After all I was sitting across from him. Google Translate fails at translating the comments accompanying the photographed dishes:

"*Now … bapmeokgi they bring before the food. Fingerfood.*
Matnapnida Bread. More than mateopeumyeon engaged ….
— Milano-style sausages.

Musun well suited for the sikgam and taste.

Now, if you ask … o … — sour —; Monte region, shrimp
and pork pie. There is a slight incline over the salt is good."

Sleep. Museum.
Risotto on a mountain (another elevator!).
Orpheum:

>Die Wellen
>Nagorny Karabach
>Dead Friends
>Let's Do it a Da Da
>Weil Weil Weil
>Unvollständigkeit
>Tagelang Weiss
>Rampe / Von wegen
>Sabrina
>Die Befindlichkeit des Landes
>Susej
>Ich warte

Graz → Zagreb.

We are royally received at the Regent Esplanade.
We are served a glass of champagne in the lobby,
which is full of formally attired people. The occasion?
I don't have the vaguest idea. German & Croatian flags
are flying in front of the hotel. The German president
is here. Servants, diplomats, bodyguards, guests of state.

We are treated with collateral grace; we are German, too. Making our way through the important guests to the elevator and to our rooms beyond is not easy. We stick out like sore thumbs. My room is a suite, and a complimentary bottle of wine on the table welcomes me. Bulletproof windows. Is the President to thank for all this, the color of my passport?

My stop in the Hotel Restaurant "Zinfandel" costs me 375 HRK, yet is, however, of no further culinary interest.

SCHEDULE	TIME
GET IN	12:00
LOAD IN	12:00
SOUNDCHECK	17:00
DINNER	18:00
DOORS	20:00
SOUNDCHECK	22:00
CURFEW	2:00

The bus encounters problems advancing to the venue. The bridges are too low. We have to take a lot of detours.

"Velika Dvorano Jedinstva":
>Die Wellen
>Nagorny Karabach
>Dead Friends

Let's Do it a Da Da
Weil Weil Weil
Unvollständigkeit
Tagelang Weiss
Rampe / Von wegen
Die Befindlichkeit des Landes
Sabrina
Susej
Ich warte

At breakfast we are reunited with yesterday's important men: they shovel food onto their plates and drink champagne like all good tourists. A German General with entourage is eating scrambled eggs at the table next to mine.

Pack rolls in napkins. Escape to the bus. Our bus is waiting in the hotel driveway outside, where leery official bodyguards gape at it distrustfully. I have no doubt that one idiot or another will be asking the usual questions: "What's the name of the band? What kind of music do they play?" for which we have pat answers ready: "Boy / Pop."

→ Budapest. Jack Weatherford: *Genghis Khan and the Making of the Modern World.*

As we did the last time, we play on a ship. Eat in the on-board restaurant. The stage and wardrobe situation below deck is rather cramped.

Die Wellen
Nagorny Karabach
Dead Friends

Let's Do it a Da Da
Weil Weil Weil
Unvollständigkeit
Tagelang Weiss
Rampe / Von wegen
Die Befindlichkeit des Landes
Sabrina
Susej
Ich warte

The television murmurs cheerful music and greets me with "Welcome, Frau Bargeld. Press Menu to Continue." Seek glasses, remote control, seek menu. Off. The cardboard sign admonishing saving disposable towels for the sake of karma is placed in front of the "stand-by" announcement. My room is full of mysterious flashing and beeping telephones. I cover the most obtrusive one with a pillow and go to bed.

At night I go out with an official delegation to visit a Hungarian atomic energy facility & test operational safety.

Magyar Energia
   we're shutting them down
         built in the '60s
Magyar Energia
   we're shutting them down
         by East Germans
Magyar Energia
   we're shutting them down
         the plants are old

Magyar Energia
we're closing them down
no longer safe

I have enough time for lunch before we depart. Restaurant "Dio" is situated near the hotel:

"*Göncoel Száraz Szamorodni 2002 Tokaj-hegyalja. Straw-yellow in color, dry wine with the delicate scent of green walnut and toasted bread. Pleasantly aromatic, with elegant oak overtones. Excellent as an aperitif.*"

Goat cheese and sour cherries, zander fillet with freshwater shrimp spread, lemon sorbet.

On the way to the bus I take a quick stab at picking up a case of Hungarian wine, Tokay, Furmit, Szürkeberat, Kékfrankos and wines from other indigenous Hungarian varietals: Mädchentraube, Kadarka. The credit card swiper is kaput. No wine.

Budapest → Vienna.

It's not all that easy to search the internet & find a place to stop and take a break on the way to Vienna while you're traveling through the Czech Republic. We stop in Brno, home to Mies van der Rohe's chair of the same name and Adolf "Ornament and Crime" Loos. The chosen restaurant is out of business. Instead: "Ristorante La Peda," which suggests Italian with empty Chianti bottles, straw flowers, and wagon wheels on the walls. There are plenty of stoats, according to the menu, even on the pizza. Stoats. The pizza pockets all have girls' names: Jana, Krystina, Michaela, and so on. Furthermore: Breaded glazed stoats. "Starobrno" Bier, Stern Brnos.

Vienna is pretty high on the list of my most visited cities, the cities where I have spent the most time, at least where German is spoken:

1. Berlin
2. San Francisco
3. Peking
4. London
5. Melbourne
6. Hamburg
7. Vienna

I once taught poetry here. I have friends here. I go out to eat with Bruno Pisek, as I usually do in Vienna.

restaurant k, early evening, dishes according to regional and seasonal availability. very simple tasting menu: everything is on the menu. i alert the waiter to our impending intoxication, as he announces a list of sixteen wines to accompany our sixteen courses.

*caramelized breast of organic drake from rohr am
        gebirge with fennel salad*
*carpaccio from peter brauchls alp lax with a gratin
        of chufa*
*jerusalem artichoke in a zucchini mantle with paradise
        apple ragout*
beef bouillon with ramps — sheeps cheese crostini
nettle foam soup with saffron butter dumplings

a duet of paprika soups with chicken-saté
red carrots with goat cheese farce and haider vineyard
    merlot butter sauce
karnten partridge with red cabbage salad
organic filet of fresh water catfish/wells with tarragon
    tender wheat berries
dornau farms lake trout baked in speck with red lentil
    ragout

I tell bruno about the luxenberg book, about the origins
of the koran in syro-aramaic — and not in arabic; about
the superimposed diacritical marks, which seem to be what
made the dark passages in the text dark. a vision of paradise
beforehand: they have wide eyed huris at their disposal,[1]
like well preserved pearls. in luxenberg's text-critical version:
white grapes, jewels like pearls. misguided hopes created
by the position of the points on the characters.

buttermilk steeped kremstal veal fillet with lemon noodles
breast of styrian pheasant stuffed with veal live with
    polenta strudel
rack of lamb from waldviertel with pretzel soufflé and
    black beer sauce
buckwheat stuffed styrian golden delicious apple
duet of chocolate pudding
let's go. the slogan: creating space. the activity: clearing out.

---

1. *Huris* is from the Arabic حُورِيَّة, DMG ḥūrīya, pl. ḥūrīyāt, and are, according to Islamic belief, virgins (al-ḥūr, "the dazzling white ones") in paradise who are assigned to the blessed.

the atmosphere: young & cheerful. we leave a final
*ringing chord in our wake.**

The taxi driver is dressed from head to toe in green:
green cap, green trousers, green shirt, green gloves.
The taxi itself is fully equipped: various lights in the
interior, for the center console, for example, to the
left an installed, retractable city map, which enables
the driver to look up the streets if he doesn't know
the way, without the passenger noticing; a speed trap
detector, etc. The whole nine yards.

"Why green?"

"Green is the color of speed."

Radisson SAS Style Hotel, Herrengasse 12. I strut
happily and alone through my hotel room.

Suggestions for the improvement of the philo-
sophic vocabulary:

Crispiness

Purée

I am simply a traveling explorer conducting
research, without a commission, specialty, or expertise.

Dürer's *Martyrdom of Ten Thousand Christians* in the
Vienna Museum of Art History, an eddy of teeming
figures. They are martyred, tortured, they plunge into
the depths. Like a time-traveler, Dürer stands with
a young friend, recently passed, distant, uninvolved,
discussing the events taking place in the center of
the picture. He fixes the observer from the picture
with his typical Dürer attitude.

In Restaurant "Novelli" the chef threatens to stop cooking unless I give him an autograph. This, at least, is what the waiter, Schmäh, asserts.

Arena. I can no longer count how often we've been here:

> Die Wellen
> Nagorny Karabach
> Dead Friends
> Let's Do it Da Da Da
> Weil Weil Weil
> Unvollständigkeit
> Tagelang Weiss
> Rampe / Von wegen
> Sabrina
> Die Befindlichkeit des Landes
> Susej
> Ich warte

A mixed drink from the hotel bar.

Vienna → Prague. In the '80s, we tried to come here to play, several times. The first time was with the assistance of a touching Czech music enthusiast; the location of our illegal concert after our arrival in Prague was to be passed on, word of mouth, by phone. We arrived late, I no longer know from where; we had broken down on some parking lot in the middle of the night. We ended up buying gas from a Turkish truck driver, which had to be sucked out of his tank using a hose (by our driver). Our driver ended up puking. So the bass player drove on. Arrival, four o'clock in the morning in the conspiratorial Prague apartment of the touching music enthusiast: Handwritten index cards with information about western bands piled everywhere, copied interviews translated into Czech. Copies of music, taped, second, third, n^{th} generation strewn about. I don't believe that arriving any earlier really would have made much of a difference as far as playing the show. It wouldn't have been possible, just in terms of the technology. There would've been a sparse crowd, anyhow.

That was our first failed attempt. Around 1983. Then, in 1987, we were asked to participate pro bono in the Olof Palme Peace March benefit concert in Munich & Pilsen (then still Czechoslovakia). We weren't the only ones. Udo Lindenberg ("I'll play for free, but my band has to be paid"), Haindling, Die Toten Hosen and a couple of other "acts"; I have fortunately forgotten the rest. The concert in Pilsen was the reason for us and for Die Toten Hosen to accept, but shortly before the Munich concert there was no more talk about the Czech concert. The German peace movement wanted to take credit for the international people's understanding, but had obviously had the clandestine plan to back off the Pilsen concert, apparently due to organizational difficulties. Only strong threats from the TH & EN yielded positive results: Pilsen was back on. Us: Hosen, Neubauten, and Haindling (No Udo) would travel on a Czech bus in the morning — meaning: unloading & reloading everything, along with the typical bickering about visas and harassment at the border. Oddly we had to spend the night in a horrid pension hotel just outside Pilsen.

(They had tried to hush up the fact that there wasn't a hotel for us in Pilsen. Thank you, Peace Movement.) The festival was to take place in a small open-air arena, on a sports field or something like that. There were Czechoslovakian bands, apparently a group from the GDR ("NO55"); various music lovers from the GDR had managed to arrive via clandestine, stealthy routes, getting off the train early before the final station to avoid the State Police, then walking the rest of the way — they managed to get that far.

Noon: Haindling performs to recorded playback, taking it easy, followed by a Czech new wave band in silver outfits, and rocks rain down (rubble from the lot!). The public hasn't come for homegrown music.

16:00: Die Toten Hosen. First encroachment by the Czech police & the East German security forces. The tension grows. In the meantime Neubauten have been killing time, drinking a lot of beer ("Pilsner Urquell"), and fraternizing with the fans. Glass breaks, doors are kicked in. I give an interview to a fanzine from the Eastern Bloc in an attic. Downstairs the brawl spills over into our dressing room area with the force of the Secret Service. Our English tour manager, a smallish woman, gets tossed around by the leathercoats. A lot of shouting. Scuffling. In the corner, unmolested: the touching Czechoslovakian music enthusiast, shaking his head, well aware of what's coming next. It takes them a while to discover me. They throw us out of our dressing area along with our instruments, cornering us to the back of the stage, where we sit around for two or three hours in an inebriated heap in the middle of musically repurposed industrial waste.

Then the decision is made: No Neubauten. Official explanation: Punk. We are stuffed into our bus surrounded by police, Stasi, & some German shepherds. The eager public is forced back.

I shout something out of window and toss a statement into the crowd; then the bus, accompanied by an officer, transports us as far as the Bavarian border: "You can walk from here!"

Years later, I'm shown the same note by a journalist at a press conference in Prague on the occasion of our first "official" concert after the Velvet Revolution:

"They don't want to let us play. They're afraid, they are afraid of you!"

Prague, 2008, Archa, subterranean:

Die Wellen
Nagorny Karabach
Dead Friends
Let's Do it a Da Da
Weil Weil Weil
Unvollständigkeit
Tagelang Weiss
Rampe / Von wegen
Die Befindlichkeit des Landes
Sabrina
Susej
Ich warte

This time I see nothing of Prague, just the Arche and the new parking garage next to it.

Prague → Warsaw, overnight. The roads aren't particularly good. Subsequently, the quality of my sleep corresponds precisely to that of the roads.

Arrival in Warsaw late in the morning: Rain, gray: Suitable. I go to Äutorska Restauracja Marty Gessler, next to the Center for Contemporary Art, eat some lunch, & from there to the club. The organizer has just moved the event here from a larger hall. It's a rathole. The worst so far. It stinks of floor wax and old beer, bad heating and yellowed files.

> Die Wellen
> Nagorny Karabach
> Dead Friends
> Let's Do it a Da Da
> Weil Weil Weil
> Unvollstandigkeit
> Tagelang Weiss
> Rampe / Von wegen
> Die Befindlichkeit des Landes
> Sabrina
> Susej
> Ich warte

Back to the hotel. People who have gambled away all their money in the casino are begging in front of the elevator. There are several prostitutes waiting in the lobby, local firms offer their services on flyers slipped under the door: Men or women, in just 10 minutes.

Even women, who have another job, are dressed like streetwalkers, whether waitresses or television anchors.

It's all about the money here, or rather, about the money that isn't here.

Room service. Breakfast. I feel nauseous all day, just enough to notice. Why? Alcohol abuse? Lack of sleep?

LO 677
From
(WAW) Frederic Chopin Airport / Warsaw, APL
to
(SVO) Sheremetyevo Airport / Moscow, RU

The flight is two hours late. My throat is coated with mucous. I order a cognac in the terminal hall, take a sip, set down the glass. Before I can take a second sip, the rim of the glass is covered with fruit flies; too late. Too many dead flies are already swimming in the glass. Disgusted, I leave the restaurant in the terminal hall and, although departure is still a long time off, go through passport and security controls to the Gate: A small room with benches all facing the tarmac. A small window marked "Drink-Bar": The cognac here is cheaper, with my last Zloty I have a second try, but the drama repeats itself; by the time I cover the glass with my passport after the first sip, there are already several files swimming in it. Drosophila melanagaster. Dew loving, black bodied flies.

Dep. Mon — Apr 21, 2008 4:05 PM
Arr. Mon — Apr 21, 2008 8:05 PM

Riots will happen, but not during take-off and landing.

I am seated right behind the curtain. First row economy, behind Business Class, where envy is at its greatest. There is no real silverware here, no real glass or china. This where they envy the space and the champagne, which nobody up front drinks, anyway. Knees grind into the back of the next seat.

For the third time: Ryszard Kapuscinski: *Imperium.*

The organizer picks us up from the airport & takes us to the hotel as usual. On my first visit to Moscow it was a hotel in Stalin's gingerbread style. The little bed sagged so much that I preferred sleeping on the floor. This time it's "Hotel President," featuring 1980s Soviet elegance, popular for third-rate conventions & second-rate guests of state. My room — or, better my rooms — are spacious, replete with vitrines filled with porcelain kitsch, featuring old-fashioned furnishings, two beds. The room service caviar now costs real money.

The organizer packs us off to a sort of sushi-disco. The New Russians love sushi, which doesn't mean that it's any good. A DJ behind the bar sets the mood for the meal. I don't like restaurants that bombard me with continual noise. A peculiar culture-fusion creation, brightly colored mixed drinks, average sushi, average saki; the prices, too, are average. Everything in Moscow is expensive. Moscow is the most expensive city in the world, followed by Tokyo. The food in Tokyo is better.

Nightcap in Hotel. Drunken German Hematologists (→ convention) & their pretty translators, slowly losing the train of thought at a round table at the hotel bar.

The warm water faucet in my bathroom falls off when I turn it. The pipes in the wall begin to groan with a loud, bass rumble. The cold water provides, according to the flow, accompaniment.

The bathwater is brownish, and the metal delivered by the pipes settles down in the bottom of the tub. The music from the porno channel rises with "Freude schöner Gotterfunken"/ "Ode to Joy."

Sleep timer: 30 minutes.

There is supposed to be a good restaurant in the Kempinski Hotel Baltschug; the 10-minute taxi ride costs €50, but the chef of this showcase restaurant has already been replaced by a less creative one. Russian menus with ox tails, smoked sturgeon, filet "Stroganoff." Foie gras, lobster, New Zealand beef, expensive garnishes, even more of the average. Expensive & silly. The service is very concerned about my apparent dissatisfaction. There's nothing they can do about it. There is a "Café Kranzler" in the Kempinski Hotel Baltschlug. There is also a "Café Kranzler" in Ajman Kempinski in Dubai. There is one in the Intercontinental in Beijing & who knows where else. I'm a Berliner and I've never set foot in Cafe Kranzler — if there even is one in Berlin anymore — and yet I still somehow manage to lead a satisfying life.

Our first concert in Moscow took place in a building that had been a Regional Cultural Center.

It smelled like rat poison; a bouquet of overcooked cabbage with an overtone of acrid ammonia — a smell that will always remind me of Moscow: sad people in mucky snow, slush, and rat poison. Real Russian mafia in dark suits as venue ushers. Uniformed neo-Nazis in the audience: Somehow, they were confused by the "German Band" thing. The usual mix-up.

In the meantime, the halls are larger, no more skinheads come to the concerts and the venue ushers are more decent. No slush, odorless rat poison. Progress.

> Die Wellen
> Nagorny Karabach
> Dead Friends
> Let's Do it a Da Da
> Weil Weil Weil
> Unvollständigkeit
> Tagelang Weiss
> Rampe / Von wegen
> Die Befindlichkeit Des Landes
> Sabrina
> Susej
> Ich warte

Russia still means the same thing: Moscow, St Petersburg. St Petersburg, Moscow. No more. Back & forth between the two overnight with the train: Caviar, borscht, blintzes, Crimean champagne and vodka in the salon wagon, a salon wagon deserving of the title.

There is a little red plastic object with a wire loop in every Pullman compartment. The passengers are instructed to use it to further secure the doors from the inside. For good reasons: One of the members of my tour was robbed, too drunk or too careless to use the additional safety lock. All the light sleepers with secured doors noticed at least one attempted break in during the night. "Ja, bitte?" Door opened. Nobody's there.

In the morning before arrival tea from the samovar and a Russian accordion version of "La Paloma" over the loudspeaker.

I ♥ night trains. I do.

This time we fly. We're playing so late in Moscow that we wouldn't arrive in St. Petersburg on time if we were to take a train. I don't fancy flying. I travel with the crew bus.

St. Petersburg: The concept here appears to be: do everything larger. That was Peter's idea. Still, the bus has difficulty getting to the hotel.

The organizer has provided me with a tourist guide and an old, black Moskva — broad back bench, white lace covers on the seats, tassels dangling in the windows (it belonged to a Party area functionary). She is cagey, and deftly bewitches the policemen who stop us for who-knows-what reasons along the way. Her business card opens even the back doors of the Hermitage. Cranach, Holbein, Caspar David Friedrich, Titian, da Vinci, El Greco, Zurbaran, Velázquez, Heda, Kalf.

The Atheist Museum no longer exists, and as we drive by it see that it's now a church again.

The Museum of the Arctic and Antarctic is exhibiting the utensils of the Soviet polar explorer who removed his own appendix with a mirror & surgical silverware.

Manege Katesgtskogo Korpusa Trinátzat, Univesitetskaya naberezhnaya — a palace right on the bank of the Neva.

Die Wellen
Nagorny Karabach
Dead Friends
Let's Do it a Da Da
Weil Weil Weil
Unvollständigkeit
Tagelang Weiss
Rampe / Von wegen
Die Befindlichkeit des Landes
Sabrina
Susej
Ich warte

The hotel is a disaster and has awarded itself four ★★★★; that's what most hotels do. At check in there is an airport style metal detector. A Canadian was recently accidentally shot in the hotel café. A beer drinking Dutch tourist group in the bar: "What's the name of the band?" "Boy." "What do you play?" "Pop."

In the hotel room I fantasize about people knocking on my door because I once danced on top of a black Mercedes Benz. That's a few years back by now; I paid for the damage, and they did not, as they had offered to, break my legs.

41

Due to the fact that I'm apparently removing my shoes too loudly, my neighbor, presumably Dutch, knocks on the wall. As a return favor, I get to hear his alarm clock go off at 4:00 AM.

St. Petersburg → Helsinki. We have never traveled this stretch, about 400 km; in the past, we never traveled by bus at all in Russia, and just a few years ago it would have been completely unthinkable. It would have been too dangerous, and the bus and its contents would never have arrived safely. Too many fake policemen along the way and — for that matter — too many real ones, too.

We have to disembark on the Russian border and walk through the passport and customs control points. It takes a while; we've arrived during the lunch break. The bus is searched. We wait.

Finland. We're in the West again, in the North to be precise, but the North here is part of the West. Euro-Land. Helsinki: Another designer hotel.

"Room categories playfully range from Mystical to Passion to Desire to Envy, all describing the emotions that are depicted from the mythical literature."

I don't know to which category my room belongs. Cæsar Salad in the restaurant. No room for more. Tavastia:

> Die Wellen
> Nagorny Karabach
> Dead Friends
> Let's Do it a Da Da

Weil Weil Weil
Unvollständigkeit
Tagelang Weiss
Rampe / Von wegen
Die Befindlichkeit des Landes
Sabrina
Susej
Ich warte

Hotel bar. Sleep.

How often have I wandered through a strange city with a hangover? Trembling, on edge and confused, until it's time for lunch, providing an excuse for one, two, three glasses of wine in this or that restaurant, bringing with it, at last, a return to alcoholic normalcy.

"Chez Dominique." In the past, it was a two ★★. What a surprise: Beautiful, modern rooms, pleasant, professional service, excellent menu:

MENU BOUILLABAISE
Marinated shellfish and rouille
Sautéed scallop, bouillabaisse consommé
Lobster and tomato
Poached turbot and spring vegetables
Popcorn and red berries

From beginning to end: Exceptional.

I am satisfied, I hadn't expected that, thinking "Chez Dominique's" cuisine would be more along the lines of old-fashioned French cuisine serving business travelers & important diners.

Helsinki-Vantaa Airport: "Finnair-Silver-Wings-Lounge," as before. Why is the wine here so bad? It's better on the Finnair flights. I've been here often in recent times. Finnair flies from Beijing to Helsinki. PEK → HEL, HEL → TXL, eight-hour flight, four hours sitting around in the lounge, then on to Berlin. The same in the reverse direction. I know the lounge, have been forced twice to waste an entire day there — missed connection due to delayed arrival. I ask the attendants about my ballpoint pen, which was lost… and then found, here ("Mont Blanc, Masterpiece"). Why hasn't it been forwarded to me?

We're off today. That means travel. In Gothenborg, being on time means that I can actually eat dinner tonight.

BOARDING PASS

			PNR		Notes					
BARGELD / BLIXA			LWOFJ		FQTV/UA			ETKT		
Flight	Date	At	Class	From	To		Gate	Seq#	Seat	Boarding
KF473	25APR	1645	M	Helsinki	Gothenburg		20B	BN44	15C	1620
Flown by	BLUE1			HEL	GOT					
Ticket number(s) 1172113803806 1 bag(s) 12Kg with tag number(s) SK 646959										

I take a taxi directly from Landvetter Airport to Sjomagasine Restaurant. The Tour manager takes my suitcase to the hotel.

A since deceased New York Times food writer described "Sjomagasinet" in Gothenborg as one of the ten culinary wonders of the world in his last column, which appeared posthumously. The face of Chef Leif Mannerstrœm graces a Swedish postage stamp. He's the ultimate authority on Matjes/pickled herring. Ten thousand guests come to his traditional Christmas dinner every year: Sixteen herring courses.

So: herring it is. I ♥ herring. And: Yes. This is really good herring.

Every variety of herring. Aquavit, then off to the hotel.

My suite features a canopy bed and yet again a welcoming bottle of wine:

A red Bordeaux. Cookies. The television is so far from the bed that I have to lift it out of its niche in the cabinet and move it onto a chair, as close as the cord will allow.

1. A comedy about television film work, the same scene is filmed over and over, whatever can go wrong, does.

2. The problems of a young woman in Hollywood — problems with her career, her mother, drugs, alcohol, showbiz, lovers, etc.

The wine has disappeared, I open the minibar: Cognac.

3. The problems of an actor on his way up and a thirty something dancer (with a child) in New York.

4. A little boy in Georgia plays golf, nothing but golf. Of course, he goes on to become world champion, the little boy from Georgia.

Bed weight attained, at last. Transmission over.
Room service: Breakfast. The lingering cold from
the tour gradually manifests itself, begging for a phar-
macist. Throat lozenges, nose drops, anti-congestants.
Welcome to Sekretia. I stay in bed until the soundcheck. I've slept through my chance to have lunch.
We don't play until 10 PM, perhaps I can still, cautiously
& light, dine before the show.

Nothing will be open afterwards. Magnus & Magnus,
Magnus 2 around the corner has a good reputation,
but is still closed when I arrive there too early.

I wait outside a few minutes until they allow me
to enter.

Abborre · Kantereller · Korngryn · Schalottenlök.
Bass · Chanterelles · Pearl barley · Shallots.

Biff · Blomkål · lök · aska.
Beef · Cauliflower · Onions · Ash

Långarygg · bönor · mandel · lakrits
Ling fillet · Beans · Almonds · Licorice

Långa? Ling? Name of fish often aren't translat-
able, and they take on different names every fifty kilometers: Carl Linnæus, himself a Swede, classified it
thus:

Kingdom: Animalia
Phylum: Chordata
Class: Actinopterygii

Order: Gadiformes
Familie: Lotidae
Genus: Molva
Species: M. molva
Molva Molva is the common name

Good food. The chef, Magnus Gunnarsson, says he's a fan. In fact, he has a CD in his car ready for an autograph (he burned it himself, interesting compilation…).
I put his name on the guest list.

  Lingon · havre · mjölk · lingonsorbet
  Lingonberries · oats · milk · lingonberry sorbet
  Die Wellen
  Nagorny Karabach
  Dead Friends
  Let's Do it a Da Da
  Weil Weil Weil
  Unvollständigkeit
  Tagelang Weiss
  Rampe / Von wegen
  Die Befindlichkeit des Landes
  Sabrina
  Susej
  Ich warte

Gothenborg → Stockholm. Autobahn construction. Large machines, each manned by a bored laborer, motionless in the sun, concentrating.

Routine sets in: The individual concerts become blurred in temporal space without lines of geographic separation, now lighter, now darker…. Where were we yesterday? Where the day before yesterday? What day is it today? Warsaw was a week ago, Russia last Wednesday: four days ago. Today's Stockholm, Sunday April 27, show day: "Berns." I ate here once a few years ago, when I had a Swedish girlfriend. It was as geriatric as the Kranzler back then. Since then it's been sold, renovated and, yes: It's impressive. We stay at the "Berns" Hotel, play in the hotel's "Stora Salongen" (chandeliers), eat in "Berns Asian" (not even all that bad), and our changing room is in the "Röda Rumet" (Strindberg's Red Room) in the hotel. A Stockholm of the short distances.

> Die Wellen
> Nagorny karabach
> Dead Friends
> Let's Do it a Da Da
> Weil Weil Weil
> Unvollständigkeit
> Tagelang Weiss
> Rampe / Von wegen
> Die Befindlichkeit des Landes
> Sabrina
> Susej
> Ich warte

Post-show drinking party with Swedish friends; actors, composers, artists.

Dror Feiler: The Bavarian Radio Orchestra doesn't want to play his commissioned composition, "Halat Hisar / State of Siege" because it's too loud.

The Director is worried about members of his orchestra suffering hearing damage.

Amanda Ooms is now the mother of twins.

Stockholm → Oslo.

Giorgio de Santillana and Hertha von Dechend: *Hamlet's Mill.*

We need to rest. The driver needs to rest. Parking lot.

A licorice shop with 400 kinds of licorice. Suspicious-looking kötbullar (meatballs).

We played the "Lakkegata Skole" in Oslo in 1983, a building used for art by the Norwegian Art Academy. Supposedly, it closed down after that. Supposedly the roof collapsed. Supposedly, supposedly. There weren't that many people there; Andrew had enough room to shoo the mob through the hall with Molotov cocktails. Power failure.

Minor revolt. We had spirited some of the instruments away from rubbish heaps and building sites, and just left it all behind after the concert. Most of them autographed (→ Akademie der Künste). Nothing exceptional. Legendary. It still gets brought up today.

I often visit Edvard Munch when I'm in Oslo, but you never know if he's at home or not. He often leaves the museum by way of the ladder, disappearing with anti-abortion activists and similar friends of the arts.

Anselm Kiefer's Lead Library, electively either *Zweistromland* or *The Empress* in Astrup Fearnley Museet

for Moderne Kunst. A room further on, paintings of
two friends: Sophie de Stempel, painted by Lucian
Freud, and Isa Genzken, painted by Gerhard Richter.

We are playing late again, time enough for me to
have dinner: "Bagatelle," I've been there before; perhaps my first meal at a Michelin-starred restaurant.
Quality. Scandinavian-French. Incomparable sea creatures from northern waters: sole from Skagerak, lobster from Kvitsoy, scallops from Tromso. Furthermore:
the usual suspects, not only on the menu — truffles,
Foie gras, etc., but also on the walls. Andreas Gursky,
Candida Hœfer, etc. Large setups at the other tables,
too: Cleptocrats, international industrialists, etc.
And me: With only a little time & a darkening mood.
It's not the chef's fault.

I receive an oyster baked with spinach as an amuse-
bouche, and order fish: I cannot nor do I want to stay
long.

St. Aubin I. Cru Clos de la Chateniere, Marc Colin
2005.

My attempts to eat are repeatedly interrupted by
a fat woman dressed in a bright orange blouse draped
with a silk scarf and a heavy bronze cross on a leather
strap. She keeps telling the others about the joys of
breastfeeding in a loud voice. The word "breastfeeding"
is stressed again and again. "Breastfeeding." What is
she? A professional wet nurse? I already know what a
man at her table dressed in a suit with metal buttons
does: He's spoken about military tanks being delivered.

Mostly, however, the "breastfeeder" is blathering on with her nerve-wracking voice; she seems to want to feed the entire restaurant, or at a minimum we are to take note of her ample, orange clad breasts, resplendent with a heavy cross.

After every loudmouthed "breastfeeding" or "you have to get your nipples out…" since "breastfeeding" is integrated in corresponding sentence contexts, she smiles at the men at the table.

Even at dessert I am interrupted again with "breastfeeding, breastfeeding, breastfeeding…"

> BELOP = 1295,00 NOK
> EXTRA = 120,00 NOK
> TOTAL = 1415,00 NOK
> TAKK FOR BESOKET
> VELKOMMEN IGJEN

"Sentrum Scene," junkie neighborhood, directly adjacent the Labor Office square, Abreidesamfunnets plass:

> Die Wellen
> Nagorny Karabach
> Dead Friends
> Let's Do it a Da Da
> Weil Weil Weil
> Unvollständigkeit
> Tagelang Weiss
> Rampe/Von wegen

Die Befindlichkeit des Landes
Sabrina
Susej
Ich Warte
Oslo → Copenhagen

Ich bin unterwegs
    I'm on the way
in einer Melange aus „Jetlag" und Alkohol
    in a melange of "jetlag" and alcohol
in einem Bus mit hundert Sachen
    in a bus at 100 km / hour

Ich bin unterwegs
    I'm on the way
mit meiner unsichtbaren Eismaschine
    with my invisible ice machine
mit meinem unsichtbaren offenen Kamin
    with my invisible open fireplace
Sie sitzen neben mir im Flugzeug
    they sit next to me in the airplane
Sie liegen neben mir in meinem „King-Size" Hotel Bett
    they lie beside me in my "king-sized" hotel bed
Sie zaehlen nicht als „Excess luggage"
    they don't count as "excess luggage"
Sie brauchen keinen „Wake-up-call"
    they don't need a "wake-up call"
Von A nach B der Liebe wegen
    From A to B because of love

Von A nach B der Liebe wegen
   From A to B because of love
Von A nach B der Liebe wegen
   From A to B because of love
Von A nach B der Liebe wegen
   From A to B because of love

The hotel in Copenhagen provides material for a lifestyle magazine. An "Ice-bar," composed completely of ice — is part of the concept. *"Just check in with one of our unique Live-life packages; enjoy life in The Wine Room, experience food and wine from all over the world; enjoy the best classical and molecular drinks served in Scandinavia in the Honey Ryder Cocktail Lounge and get a cool experience in the exceptional Absolut Icebar Copenhagen, built uniquely with ice from the Torne-River in Lapland. Even the restrooms are designed to give you an extraordinary experience."*

What, pray, is a "Live-life package"? What are molecular drinks? Whatever.

I can find no indication of how to operate my phone, or instructions of how to do so, in the extremely small room. What do I dial to connect to the reception? It's usually "9" or "0," but not here. I find the hotel phone number on a brochure left in the room and dial it on my cell phone. Unfortunately, I reach the central booking office for the entire chain, which isn't even located in Copenhagen and doesn't know what number to dial, either. So — down I go, down to the lobby to speak directly to the receptionist:

She is ensconced behind a sort of sideboard, anything else would be too old-fashioned. She looks very Danish behind the shelves of brightly lit packaged sandwiches and soft drinks. When it's my turn — I have to wait a while to speak with her — it takes her a bit to understand my problem. Or rather, she doesn't understand it and considers it *my* problem, which by now is really pushing *my* buttons, somewhat. No matter. No time: I cut off her declaration with a wave of my hand. "I don't really want to discuss this with you. All I want is a reservation for Bo Beck's restaurant for lunch, for one, for now. Can you do that?" "I don't feel like it." "What?" Several curious onlookers have gathered behind us, among them, fortunately, my tour manager. I leave further discussion to him, get into a taxi and call "Bo Beck at Restaurant Partisan" while already on the way there.

A restaurant in a furniture showroom in the North Harbor Docks almost outside Copenhagen. There are four menu choices.

> *Chlorophyll*
> *The vegetarian menu*

Magnificent, but not today...

> *Brillat-Savarin*

Maybe...

> *Lunch*
> *Two light courses, different every day*

No. I don't need that. I have time.

The Alchemist
The surprise menu
Forward mindset with respect for the classic kitchen

Yep, that's it. Surprise me. More than half a dozen happily and successfully whimsically culinary bagatelles arrive in succession, and indeed, I am pleasantly surprised.

I don't know if Bo Beck has studied under Feran Adrià in Roses or if he thought up these techniques on his own, but it works; it's not a bunch of silliness. Even the main courses:

Poached King crab with hazelnut oil marzipan &
    cauliflower mosaic
Grilled leek marrow with horseradish & flat parsley
Raw fried lobster with gelled green peas & cress
Lemon sole with soft nuances of tomato & garlic
Oxidized mushroom bouillon

The menu description doesn't begin to convey what he creates and how he presents the dishes. The ingredients glow.

The waiter is unobtrusive and polite. Not even the other diners are unpleasant. The menu is probably too modern for businessmenski. Material for molecular cuisine jokes? Mistake: Cheery.

Smoked creamy chocolate with porous lavender bobbles
Cognac "Paradis extra" Hennessy

I ride back to the hotel, endorphenized, naturally only to pick up my suitcase. After the earlier display I'm not staying here. The contents of my suitcase have been dumped out on the bed; the suitcase lies beside them. My laptop blinks within, completely unimpressed. It appears that someone climbed through the window, situated not far above the terrace, to steal the computer, which can be seen blinking from outside, and probably anything else worth the effort. He/she then gathered the router, earphones, and hardware in the suitcase. I don't know why s/he didn't complete her/his project. Was the suitcase too awkward? Too obvious? Too heavy? Did someone see her/him ? Did they think they were being observed? Did I arrive too early?

What do I know...

I check into a hotel by City Hall around the corner.

We're off today. I've already arrived, don't need to go anywhere, and if I drop my laundry at the reception desk, I will have clean clothes tomorrow. We are rarely in one place long enough, and there won't be another opportunity before Barcelona.

Siesta.

Once, our electric hammer disappeared from the car one night in Copenhagen.

We had played in "Üngdomhuset," a popular, squatted building. Andrei "Ornament und Verbrechen"

Unruh was hanging suspended somewhere beneath the stucco ceiling and had undertaken some architectural improvements with the electric hammer. Squatters are by and large pretty conservative people; they could or would not share N.U.'s æsthetic point of view. Result: Four punctured tires, the van's windshield shattered, various articles disappeared, among them the aforementioned Kango-Hammer. We never owned a jackhammer, contrary to popular assertion.

In 2007 the same Üngdomhuset requests permission to use a piece from the very same concert for their benefit compilation CD. Sure. I suggest a title: "Where's our Kango-Hammer?" They hint that something might be able to be done about it.

One multi-course tasting meal a day is sufficient. I have a cheese plate sent up to my room and watch TV.

Wander mit dem Finger [2]
  Wander with a finger
Durch alle Kanäle
  Through all channels
Und finde nichts
  And find nothing
Dafür gibt es ein Wort
  There's a word for that

2. This is part of a lyric from "Nocturnalie" by Teho Teardo & Blixa Bargeld, a song from the album *Still Smiling*, which was released in 2013, just a few years after this book/tour.

Auch dafür gibt es ein Wort
> There's a word for that too

Der Lieder sinken gravitätisch zusammen
> The songs sink gravitationally together

Der Film verläuft sich ohne mich
> The film runs without me

Was der Mund verzahnt wird noch geputzt
> Which the toothed mouth is still being cleaned

Umlaufbahn
> Orbit

Sektengelände, utopischer Ort:
> Sectarian site, utopian place:

Jeder hat sein eigenes Haus
> Everyone has his own house

Shakespeare is dort
> Shakespeare is there

Es wird mit verrotteten Lilien gedüngt
> Fertilized with rotten lilies

Dafür gibt es ein Wort
> There's a word for that

Meine Hände werden deiner Haut nicht satt
> My hands never grow tired of your skin

Meine Mitte will nicht
> My center will not

An deiner statt, die Hände
> In your place, hands

Ohne Möbel ohne Wände
> Without furniture without walls

Auf dem Boden auf der Flucht
    On the floor on the run
Dafür gibt es ein Wort
    There's a word for that
Dafür gibt es ein Wort
    There's a word for that

"Noma" sounds like a museum, but it is really the abbreviation for "Nordatlantisk Mad," North Atlantic Foods, a restaurant that only uses ingredients from Nordic countries. It's pleasantly bright & spacious, the headwaiter is very proud of their recent rating as 10th best restaurant on the San Pellegrino list. Last year they were 18th. Of course, I choose the sampler menu:

Razor clams & horseradish "snow"
Parsley & dill

Salsify & milk skin
Rapeseed oil & truffle from Gotland

Turbot & watercress
"Kodrivere" & ramson onion

Onions from Laeso
Onion-cress & onion bouillon

Pork from Dronningmolle & leek
Malt, seeds & fresh leaves of acidic herbs

Roasted Jerusalem artichoke & iced sea buckthorn
Vinegar & malt

Dried berries & dried cream
Walnuts & dust of walnuts

A restaurant with razor clams on the menu served with foam also can definitely be included on my personal "Best of" list.

Behind me at the side table sits a couple with expensive cameras are painstakingly photographing every course. They aren't food bloggers. They are pros: food porn writers, San Pellegrino critics, something of the sort. They are served by the Chef and owner, Rene Redzepi himself. Important people: Vapid chatter, glasses are held up to the light, the reflections admired. They rhapsodize over summer evenings on the Loire. When the Chef is out of hearing range and back in the kitchen again, the meal is reviewed very skeptically: He doesn't like buttermilk, no raisins, just the big ones, finds it all much too simple. She finds the service too relaxed for a restaurant of this caliber. Bla-Bla-Bla-barricades.

Why does this always happen to me?

Of all the restaurants I've visited during this tour, I like this one best — better even than yesterday.

Copenhagen, a surprise. Barcelona still lies ahead. René's kitchen is inventive. Good. Without concession. Precisely those dishes he prepares with extremely simple ingredients are magnificent: An entremets combining 12 different plants of the alum family, Rams = Allium Ursinum = Ramps, Leeks from somewhere up north, special onions from Laes. The restaurant employs 12 foragers to assure a continuous supply for these special dishes. I leave a note expressing my respect for the kitchen. I don't do that often.

1ST LOBBY CALL BAND: 4:45 PM
2ND LOBBY CALL BAND: 5:30 PM

For my voice: Calcium — Sandoz, 9 mg Ca/ml, inject, Calc. glubion., 5 amp á 10 ml.

Store Vega (Main Hall). The security guard watching our dressing room is studying a textbook on internal medicine.

Die Wellen
Nagorny Karabach
Dead Friends
Let's Do it a Da Da
Weil Weil Weil
Unvolstaendigkein
Tagelang Weiss
Rampe / Von wegen
Die Befindlichkeit des Landes
Sabrina
Susej
Ich Warte

Remove makeup. Lie down.

Out of the blue I've received an Oscar. (For what, actually? For which film? As an actor? For film music?)

I am unprepared for the ensuing commotion. My hair is messed up, and I am not wearing anything but a shirt. I hastily pull on a pair of black sweatpants for the first photos up on the podium. I don't make a good impression ... does it matter?

Envy and malice abound. The German media are almost bitter, not to mention the stars and starlets.

This is starting to be fun.

I get a haircut, go shopping, am fawned over.

I have, after all, been awarded an Oscar.

Ciproxin® 250 mg, Ciprofloxacin 10 tabl.
Hexocain®, lozenges 20 pc.
Claritin® 10 mg, Loratadin 10 pills
Iliadin®, 0.5 mg/ml, 10 ml nasal spray

My abyss, as usual, ends with pharmaceutical realism.

Breakfast room, it's being renovated ...

The little butter packets, which I can't open neatly, the corner I can't quite grasp.

There is only green tea here with added flavors. OK: Peppermint may be tolerable ...

One table over, someone is selling the winter sport of the future for ski resorts sabotaged by "global warming," a sort of skiing on wheels, "Skiing," also called "Nordic Blading." He sells know-how and equipment, prices, poles, Skikes, certified trainers, training camps and other things, in general, the future.

Enough Nordic-ness. Travel day. I.E.: We fly. Westwards.

→ Airport Copenhagen Check in (141)

→ Security (8) → Terminal 2

B Gates → British Airways Lounge (A Gates)

→ Caviar House Seafood Bar (A Gates) … try on a pair of shoes along the way… → British Airways Lounge (A Gates) → Gate A 18 → Airplane → Seat 8 C … Seat is broken → Seat 8 D.

As usual I have a vision of us in the ocean next to the gaping fuselage of a downed plane.

Mark Kurlansky: *Cod. The Fish that Changed the World*

Arrival Porto 20:10
Porto Palacio Hotel, port wine on the roof.

| VIP Lounge Bebidas | 01.05 | 50.50 |
| #1717: Check #6198 | | |

| VIP Lounge Tips | 01.05 | 5.00 |
| #1717: Check #6198 | | |

Elaborate breakfast. Excellent Chinese green tea.

Porto: View from the cathedral of the Port wine bank on the other side of the Douro River.

```
                    DOW'S
                              BARROS
          OFFLEY
                                        WARRE
DELAFORCE
     CROFT          RAINHA SANTA
                              SANDEMAN

     SANDEMAN

NOVAL
```

Lunch at "D. Tonho." *Bacalhau gomes Sa* — salted cod, reconstructed, ex mummified fish. I ♥ Bacalhau.

"Casa Da Mùsica," "House of Music":

Die Wellen

Nagorny Karabach

Dead Friends

Let's Do it a Da Da

Weil Weil Weil

Unvollständigkeit

Tagelang Weiss

Rampe / Von wegen

Die Befindlichkeit des Landes

Sabrina

Susej

Ich warte

Porto → Lisbon

Sunday, busy seafood restaurant. Marine creatures for the entire family. Paper tablecloths, shrimp, Vinho Verde. I have ample time after lunch for observing people, street vendors, their bosses who linger nonchalantly in the background or step up as customers appear… Who buys these kinds of shirts? The salesman doesn't shout, he babbles in monotone, smokes, fumbles around with his merchandise now & then, unfolding or folding this shirt or that. They're ugly, the shirts, and unattractively displayed to boot — just dumped out onto a plastic tarp.

When the police drive up — it's a pedestrian zone — the tarp is hastily pulled back and folded over, as if they were just about to leave; the boss — gold rings, black shirt — greets them through the car window with an exaggerated grin; the police drive on, the tarp is once again spread out, the sales begin again, and they actually sell two shirts.

There is an astounding number of handicapped people here. People with tubes in their noses, abscesses on their faces, arms in slings, crutches & so on. I even witness a fit. Walking around before lunch, I hear screams. A hysterical woman runs onto the street, the door flung open. I remain a few moments longer. Screaming, she sits down on a short stone wall that runs along the street. She tears continuously at her hair, stopping now and then to shred her clothing, pulling it down from her breasts and beating them dramatically with her fists. A gesture that suggests that they aren't there or are no longer there. What's going on here? A mugging? Murder? Serious domestic conflict? Violence? I can't tell what the woman is screaming, but she's obviously doing it to get attention, and after a while they come, from a courtyard behind a driveway at the end of the street — curious onlookers & first aid: They're mostly Muslims wearing caps. Standing a few meters away, dressed in black, obviously a foreigner, suspicious, I feel uncomfortable. I'd almost prefer to turn around and walk down the mountain. Who knows what's going on here. But I need to go in the opposite direction, I think, so I keep walking toward the quickly gathering mob, past the open door of the house in question. An older man in a wheelchair is just being pushed outside. Perhaps he suffered some sort of seizure or attack; at least he's still alive... quite honestly, it looks more as if the screaming woman in the street is having some sort of attack & not the trembling old man. The passage at the end of the street turns out to be the driveway to a hospital, which makes all the sense in the world. They won't have to push the wheelchair very far. To the left, a narrow alley leads back down the hill. It wouldn't surprise me if I were to be attacked from behind while climbing down the stairs. I almost expect to be, I don't know exactly what's going on here, and I'm suspicious, almost meta-physically suspicious. Who's that man? What's he doing here? A bringer of bad fortune, perhaps Death himself.

Aula Magna, the University:

Die Wellen
Nagorny Karabach
Dead Friends
Let's Do it a Da Da
Weil Weil Weil

Unvollständigkeit
Tagelang Weiss
Rampe / Von wegen
Die Befindlichkeit des Landes
Sabrina
Susej
Ich warte

The next morning I want to go to Sintra before our departure. I get up at 7:00 AM and take a taxi to the most western point in all of Europe: A cliff. The horizon, the sky, the same colors.

Der Regenspazierer
  The rainwalker
an der Küste
  on the coast
einen Schirm hat er gekauft
  an umbrella that he bought
und vergessen
  and forgot
sein Herz daran zu hängen
  to hang his heart on it
im Taxi klamm
  in the cab clammy
der Ausflug war
  the trip was
ohne Worte
  without words
wie der Schlaf
  like sleep

Lisbon → Malaga.

We stop at Vila Real de Santo Antonio on the Algarve Coast before we reach the Spanish border. Seafood & wine.

We arrive late in Malaga. Very late. No sound check, no time to go to the hotel first. The bus driver has trouble finding "Teatro Cervantes." He encounters difficulties maneuvering the bus through the old town. The police stop us, and after some back & forth they finally escort the bus to the stage door. Change of clothes underway, make up underway, in the swaying bus bathroom. We're on in 10 minutes. For the first time in my life: Out of the bus → onto the stage. A cosmic blackness before me. A dark void. The void applauds.

> Die Wellen
> Nagorny Karabach
> Dead Friends
> Let's Do it a Da Da
> Weil Weil Weil
> Unvollständigkeit
> Tagelang Weiss
> Rampe / Von wegen
> Die Befindlichkeit des Landes
> Sabrina
> Susej
> Ich warte

Hotel. I don't see where I've ended up until I open the curtains in the morning. The window opens to a view over the marina, the harbor, to the Mediterranean.

I've never been here. It's still early, but we have more than a thousand kilometers to Barcelona. Pity. It's lovely here.

Aeorporto de Malaga. Terminal Pablo Ruiz Picasso. Signage in three languages: Spanish, German, English. No wonder: Costa del Sol. Only as minority of the passengers come here on business. It's sticky and close. Too many people, too many delays. Clickair XG 1035, Departure 09:10, 26D. My aisle seat turns out to be a window seat. Economy: Just don't give in to claustrophobia; don't think of the narrow space. Diversion: Headphones, "The Simpsons" on the computer, white wine through to Barcelona.

987 Barcelona Hotel. A "design hotel," no surprise. Good neighborhood. "Comida" around the corner: "Lasarte Restaurante" (Direcion Martin Berasategui).

Martin Berasategui is the chef of the eponymous Restaurant near San Sebastian in Basque Country. This is his Catalan branch. Menù degustaciò.

Pear, tomato confit, royal crab, sprouts & apple juice

*Sea urchin & razor curd cream, salted sprouts,
Seaweed, with coffee & curry cappuccino*

*Free range eggs with beetroot, liquid grass salad,
Pork belly carpaccio, vacherin & morilles*

*Line Fish, fideuda without pasta, seaweed, wedge clams,
Orange carbon oil & light "al i oli"*

Rabbit civet cannelloni, fois gras curd, wine,
Apple compote & orange sand

Pineapple raw & roasted with sate, coconut, & lime

Creamy chocolate & Clementine, cocoa sand
& various raspberries

"Petit-fours"
Muskovado financier · Rose jelly mint chocolate
Tiramisu Xoff

Siesta, interview in the hotel bar. Sala Apolo:
    Die Wellen
    Nagorny Karabach
    Dead Friends
    Let's Do it a Da Da
    Weil Weil Weil
    Unvollständigkeit
    Tagelang Weiss
    Rampe / Von wegen
    Die Befindlichkeit des Landes
    Sabrina
    Susej
    Ich warte
Day off. Beginning now, we have four free days.
The band scatters, some fly home, others stay here.
We've rented an apartment in "El Born," an old, now
very popular Barcelona quarter. My wife is here, friends
are here. It's raining. It rains a lot, so much that it
causes problems for Catalonia.

Languages in Prehistoric Europe and Europa Semetica
by Theo Vennemann. Europe after the Ice Age, Basque
Europe.

Alicia Framis is a Catalonian artist with a residence
in Shanghai: she has emailed me, or rather my office,
"blitzmail," texted to ask for my cooperation for her
next exhibition. The first part of a large project titled:
"Welcome to Guantanamo Museum."

I am to lend my voice to an "Audio Installation" in
this hypothetical museum. A list of prisoners prepared
rhythmically and associatively for me by Enrique Villa-
Matas. A speech coach has been arranged for me —
the names are Arabic — and a recording studio in
a Barcelona suburb. Headphone feedback, loose
connections, ancient equipment, but it works:

     "Mohammad
     Muhammed
     Abu Shaker
     Amer
     Ahmed
     Mahmud
     Kareem
     Amr
     Abdul Mani
     Yaser
     Ali
     Omar
     Tarek
     Mazen

Nadim
Shah David
Salim
Mohamed, Ali, Abdul…

Sufyian
Ahmad
Fawzi
Gholam
Asif
Rhunhel
Sofiane
Wallid
Ibrahim
Mustafa
Adel
Ben Ismail
Sassi
Said
Mesut
Abdallah Aiza
Mullah
Fahed
Nasser
Mohamed, Ali, Abdul…

Zia
Hijaz
Uthman

Feroz
Muaz
Faruq
Ibrahim
Idris
Mujahid
Ali
Majid
Abdel
Sayf
Abdulah
Assem
Sultan
Omar
Yahya
Njeb
Yusif
Mohamed, Ali, Abdul…

Sadiq
Laacin
Mehrabamb
Habib
Salam
Mubarak
Hussain
Khalid
Fayiz
Martin
Sabir

Boudella
Lakhdar
Hassan
Shakhrukh
Majeed
Uthman
Muaz
Hamza
Matruq
Mohamed, Ali, Abdul…"

We had to remove a few prisoners from the list. They either slipped in or the names were recorded incorrectly, one of them was "Schmid." Schmid in Guantanamo? I hope I won't experience problems reentering the United States. Homeland Security searched my computer the last time. As a precaution, I'll make sure to delete all emails on the subject.

We're done in a few hours. Tarik Omauri, my voice trainer, is satisfied. Arriving back in Barcelona, Alicia invites us for paella near the old harbor. Fortunately, it's not raining right now.

For the evening we've managed to get a table at "El Bulli," which borders on a miracle or is just down to having very influential friends, since "El Bulli" only takes reservations one day a year for the entire year, and then only for a few hours. Our table is reserved for 10:30 PM. 10:30 PM? In a restaurant that only does one set of guests a night? Which serves 30, naturally very small, courses?

"El Bulli" is in Roses, in the Gulf of Roses, beautifully situated on a mountainside overlooking the coast. This much we know, but just not the best way to get there.

When we call the restaurant to inquire, we discover that our table is actually reserved for 8 PM, and that no guests are seated after 9. It's 7 PM. 7 PM! Taxi! Barcelona → Roses: 167 km. Unfortunately, the taxi driver is neither an aficionado of Spanish *haute gastronomie* nor a native of the Gulf of Roses, which turns the drive against time into a nerve-jangling undertaking. We call the restaurant repeatedly and hand the phone to the taxi driver so that he can report his latest position and the nearest street signs. We arrive at the restaurant at a quarter past nine. The taxi ride costs more than the 30-course menu. Inside everyone is cordial, taking great pains to put us at ease. We must make a frantic impression. Everything's fine, we're not too late, and are asked if we'd like to see the kitchen.

Of course, we would. It's true: The number of cooks in the kitchen is about equal to the number of guests, with a magnificent, nearly soundless bustling about: They're all very young, very international, will probably return to their respective countries after their apprenticeships to hoist the flag of their master in new restaurants. Ferran Adrià is standing alone at the stainless steel island in front and supervises the activity; the succession of courses. The business has electronic organizers with records for each guest, so they know who has been served what at any given moment, what they liked or rejected. No one ever eats the same meal twice in El Bulli. Ferran Adrià has a second restaurant in Valencia which serves only his greatest hits with the item's year noted on the menu: "Gin Fizz" 1998, "Peas" 2001; here, however, he only prepares the latest program (although "DOCUMENTA KASSEL 16/06 – 23/09 2007 is still imprinted on the menu — just as a memento, as the Maître D assures us). "The latest album" of 2008 is everything that he and his team have developed in the lab during the half-year in which the restaurant is closed.

yuzu / sake / Kyoto
nori — Trias
spherical olives
tomato cookie
pine kernel & chocolate bonbons
beetroot & yoghurt meringue
rabbit ear crunchie
mint leaf
strawberries
gorgonzola moshi
black sesame sponge cake with miso
flowers paper
cream-LYO
asparagus with miso
razor clams / Laurencia
haricot bean with Joselito's Iberian pork fat
tangerine flower / pumpkin oil with mandarin seeds
almonds jelly with cocktail of fresh almonds "Umeboshi"

anchovy & ham with yoghurt yuba
water lily
peas 2008
sea anemone 2008
gnocchi of polenta with coffee & safran yuba
sea cucumber with mentaiko & rhubarb
"negrito" 2008
game meat canapé
hare juice with apple jelly-cru with black currant marinated
brie stuffed with truffels
"trufitas"
Lulo
Morphings…

Has Ferran been soaking up inspiration in Japan? The evening is full of Japanese ingredients and consistencies: Yuzu (a Japanese citrus), Nori (sea algae), Moshi (shrimp rice balls), Yuba (soymilk skin), Mentaiko (marinated fish roe) and miso. Flowers pressed in edible papers, sea anemonæ in bonsai garden pong landscapes. As expected: the entertainingly unexpected. No vacuous effects. Also astounding: Almost no meat. A rabbit ear, a bit of ham…. "El Bulli" is the best restaurant in the world; I am on the waiting list for the second best, Heston Blumenthal's Fat Duck in Berkshire in England. Copenhagen surprised me; from Catalonia — there are after all nearly a dozen restaurants in the same league here — I expected this much culinary inventiveness, this much class.

Everything is new, newly conceived, reinvented backwards, new tastes, new ideas. Just a moment. I've actually already eaten the spherical olives, in Valencia, in the "Greatest Hits" restaurant. That's what made him famous. Doesn't matter. Still good.

A second taxi takes us back to Barcelona. Satisfied.

Barcelona → Lyon, 7:30 AM

I get on the bus. I, my small suitcase, my garment bag, my computer bag. I'm the only passenger. The others flew yesterday.

After a short chat with the bus driver and a cup of tea I lie down in my berth. We've left Barcelona, are traveling north on the freeway to Francia.

We'll be traveling for about eight hours, so perhaps stop once to eat something, but after the culinary excesses in Barcelona I don't really feel like it.

We drive straight through. Stop to refuel — but otherwise in one stretch. "Hilton Lyon," I've been here before. A modern construction strip on the banks of the Rhone, Quai Charles de Baule. Block after block: hotels, restaurants, casinos. A new pedestrian zone in "Parc de la tête d'or," the park of the golden head. I go into one of the French bistro simulations, order cheese, water, & a "Negroni"; the waitress recognizes me, but the man at the bar has no "Negroni":

Gin
Sweet Vermouth
Campari

We are playing at a venue within walking distance, "Boulevard de Stalingrad," last block on the same bank, multi-use hall, cultural, new construction.

> Die Wellen
> Nagorny Karabach
> Dead Friends
> Let's Do it a Da Da
> Weil Weil Weil
> Unvollständigkeit
> Tagelang Weiss
> Rampe / Von wegen
> Die Befindlichkeit des Landes
> Sabrina
> Susej
> Ich warte

Without incident.

Lyon → Paris

Paris by train. I want to accept the award for my life's work afterwards.

> TGV 613
> VOITURE 03
> PLACE ASSISE 46
> OI COULOIR
> DUPLEX: EN BAS

Lunch invitation in "Cour Jardin" of "Hotel Plaza Athénée," the award is presented, a cylinder filled with quartz crystals —, photos are taken, saffron risotto, in Bouillabaisse broth, champagne, Alexandre Grauer, "President" of the "Quartz Electronic Music Awards," nice man.

Before I set out for "Venue" I pass by Guerlain on the Champs Élysées: "Bois d'Arménie" can only be bought here: incense, wood, and a little hint of iris in the head; coriander, rose pepper, and benzoin in the long breath; a heart of patchouli. Faded memories of Indian shops in the 70s. Somewhere, far in the background, a rose. Androgynous. Everything fits.

We have played at "Bataclan" repeatedly since the introduction of volume limits for concerts, in other locations the implementation was worse, stricter, unbearable. It's OK here. The way the volume is measured here (in decibels, a logarithmic ratio) doesn't really help. Any orchestra playing fortissimo would exceed the specified limits. Or, as we were able to demonstrate once in the "Élysée Montmartre": One beat on our metal plates is louder than the French government permits even with the amplifiers turned off. We are not all that loud. We can hear the cell phones in the first row. The dressing room in "Bataclan" is as large as a bath towel and not at all suitable for socializing; I find a seat in a bistro, drink wine and read.

Lewis Hyde: *Trickster Makes This World*

Now and then I autograph a t-shirt, a CD, or an arm. When I get ready to leave, I learn that fans in the restaurant have paid my bill without making a fuss about it.

Die Wellen
Nagorny Karabach
Dead Friends
Let's Do it a Da Da
Weil Weil Weil
Unvollständigkeit
Tagelang Weiss
Rampe / Von wegen
Die Befindlichkeit des Landes
Sabrina
Susej
Ich warte
Paris → Frankfurt am Main
Antique automobiles in the hotel lobby.
Smoking under palm trees.
Cold yogurt soup €3.50
Offenbach. Capitol:
Die Wellen
Nagorny Karabach
Dead Friends
Let's Do it a Da Da
Weil Weil Weil
Unvollständigkeit
Tagelang Weiss
Rampe / Von wegen
Die Befindlichkeit des Landes
Sabrina
Susej
Ich warte

With Rudi at the hotel bar. Jolly liquor guessing-games with the barkeep.

From Mokkum Pey to Godel Mokkum Hey (The big city of Hamburg).

HH / Hbf. / Junky-Sputumregen → Lange Reihe:

"Sgroi." Lunch menu + baked figs. Last year, when sinus problems prevented me from flying, Anna Sgroi prepared my travel provisions: Culatello di Zibello, olives, fresh bread, wine, glass & corkscrew. The first ham since my childhood — I was a vegetarian/pesca-tarian for 30 years. I've only been an omnivore since Beijing — a happy, solitary meal with Bertolucci's *Il Conformista* in the Pullman to Genoa.

A bottle of white wine to take back to the hotel.

In the evening, Rocko Schamoni in the Schau-spielhaus:

It's funny after all these years. Zadek — Andi — wild days, hard nights, back in 1987.

And now meeting Schamoni again. Is he still on speed? That'd be funny. How do I look, do I have my stool with me?

Down the stairs, around the corner, past the counter, everything as usual.

Well well, there he is. Should I hug him when I greet him?

I just put my hand on his head. Where is my stool? Oh, here, so sit down. He's wearing mirrored glasses. What's the point of that? Never mind, I can look at myself. The way he looks at me — is he still in love? What's he talking about? Nonsense, I don't listen at all, I just make hints in between.

*Is he going to go play footsies under the table? I look at myself
in his mirrored glasses: I look good. Schamoni's nose is red, he
talks loudly, quickly, confusedly, the sentences burst forth like
confused little horses driven by waves of spit. He's on a roll. Still,
I relish the situation, the scent of his body is just incomparable,
the drugs & stress creating an extremely original scent of sweat
with shimmering combative sequences, a plume of peanut oil
and a deep, catty bass note. It's worth coming for that alone.*

*I notice him perusing me with his half-concealed eyes and
decide to conclude our brief interlude so as not to get his hopes
up after all. After a brief but very tender tongue-lashing, I leave.**

Around the corner here, in the Schmilinskystraße,
we once lived in an apartment on the ground floor,
Alex & I. Back in the Schauspielhaus days.

We were in Hamburg a lot, we recorded records here;
they were called records back then. Our first concert
outside of Berlin was at the "Markthalle": A hail of beer
bottles, cat calls. Mobbing local chauvinist punks, like
everywhere in Wessi-land at that time.

Ich wünsch mir 'ne neue Blockade …
I want a new blockade …
    Ich wünsch mir 'ne neue Blockade …
    I want a new blockade …
        Ich wünsch mir 'ne neue Blockade …
        I want a new blockade …
            … für Ber-lin
            … for Ber-lin

A couple more glasses of wine in "Cox" and then back to the hotel.

Title of my next solo album: "Songs about Depression that Make Other People Laugh."

Laeiszhalle, not for the first time, a beautiful concert hall:

> Die Wellen
> Nagorny Karabach
> Dead Friends
> Let's Do it a Da Da
> Weil Weil Weil
> Unvollständigkeit
> Tagelang Weiss
> Rampe / Von wegen
> Die Befindlichkeit des Landes
> Sabrina
> Susej
> Ich warte

Full house, full dressing room, friends, acquaintances, relatives. Rocko sends his apologies per SMS: He had an accident in the canteen of the Schauspielhaus, so he went to the North Sea Coast.

TRAVEL:
Band leaves Hamburg in the morning for Leipzig

NOTES:
1ST LOBBY CALL BAND 10:30 AM
2ND LOBBY CALL BAND: NONE
390 KM

Not a lot has stuck from Hamburg this time. Saw Rocko briefly the evening before, then Matthew (Partridge, my translator), Fritz (Brinkmann, creator of various album covers), Peter (Sempel, filmmaker).

Who else? Where did I eat, actually?

Haus Auensee, Leipzig. The weather is lovely, most of the audience is hanging around in the park. Before the concert starts, I have Andrew push me around outside in a shopping cart, armed with a megaphone, thus herding the people into the hall at the top of my voice.

Intro / Die Wellen
Nagorny Karabach
Dead Friends
Let's Do it a Da Da
Weil Weil Weil
Unvollständigkeit
Tagelang Weiss
Rampe / Von wegen
Die Befindlichkeit des Landes
Sabrina
Susej
Ich warte

Odd hall, nice concert. Afterwards, as always, a short "hello" from "Prince" Sebastian Krumbiegel. In front of the hotel: beer ad with "Prince" Sebastian Krumbiegel. The entire band in the modern hotel bar. There's nothing more to eat.

On to Munich by train. Lunch in Tantris. Tantris looks magnificent — I think it was recently renovated.

The colors, the carpeted walls — restored. The '70s
never looked as good as here. A culinary sacred bunker.
A lone diner, I'm seated in the middle of the room.
Lunch menu:

Lauwarmer Saibling
mit Tartar, weissem Spargel und Mousse

*

Gebratener Seeteufel mit Hummer,
Spinat und Olivennudeln im Sud

*

Gratinierte Lammnuss mit Bohnen,
Bak choy und Auberginenpürée

*

Milchrahmstrudel mit Erdbeeren
und Topfen-Vanilleeis

At a table near a window, too close not to be over-
heard, a group of three: in school English, German,
and American, they are discussing the script for a still-
to-be-produced film with a young American director
for a new product for artificial nutrition in hospitals.
The filmmaker finds the text — which he obviously
doesn't understand, since it is targeted to medical
professionals and written in their technical language
— too complicated. He repeatedly tries to dumb it
down, but is repeatedly dissuaded from doing so by the
author, an old medical doctor, along with the young
German, who is a representative of the production

company or the pharmaceutical company, because of the errors and inconsistencies in the content that could arise as a result.

The scientific term for the absorption of nutrients into the bloodstream cannot be replaced by "to break up" or "to decompose," as he suggests: the latter is clear at my table. The only technical term he doesn't want to remove is "intravenous"; as a slogan he wants to use: "for people who can't eat normally" or "until they can eat normally again," which obviously doesn't inspire any enthusiasm on the part of his business partners. He himself is only eating salad.

Cab to the hotel.

A ray of sunlight in the form of a glowing streptococci wanders across the blood count of my bedsheet.

Muffathalle:

Die Wellen
Nagorny Karabach
Dead Friends
Let's Do it a Da Da
Weil Weil Weil
Unvollständigkeit
Tagelang Weiss
Rampe / Von wegen
Die Befindlichkeit des Landes
Sabrina
Susej
Ich warte

Munich → Cologne. Our bus breaks down between
Biebelried and Theilheim. I know nothing about motor
vehicles: Nothing works anymore. We call four cabs
from the next town and drive to the Würzburg main
station, from there, after loitering together at a fish
sandwich stand, we take the train to Cologne. No time
for the hotel, immediately to E-Werk. We've played
here a dozen times since it opened in 1991. In the
meantime, it has become quite run-down:

> Die Wellen
> Nagorny Karabach
> Dead Friends
> Let's Do it a Da Da
> Weil Weil Weil
> Unvollständigkeit
> Tagelang Weiss
> Rampe / Von wegen
> Die Befindlichkeit des Landes
> Sabrina
> Susej
> Ich warte

At the closing announcement, someone throws
an old piece of chewing gum in my face (Danke!).
Afterwards, backstage: drunken Neue Deutsche Welle
factotums.

Let's get the fuck out of here.

In the hotel bar we have a drink with Bruno & friends.

This has been a Sunday replete with accumulating
mutations ...

Cologne → Amsterdam, 212 km, a travel day.

Festive dinner for the entire staff at the "Restaurant Amsterdam," a former pump house, in Amsterdam: tour manager, production manager, sound engineer, lighting technician, monitor engineer, technician, guitar technician, documentarian, shirt and souvenir salesman, bus drivers, truck drivers, musicians.

Fish soup with rouille & crouton
Dutch herring
Steamed mackerel & toast
Dutch shrimps with lemon mayonnaise
Mussels, French fries, salad
Warm apple pie with ice cream & cream

A Tour group-photo on the stairs to the restaurant.

Afterwards, everyone disperses into the Amsterdam night, the coffee shops, and to enjoy other pleasures or goes to sleep, finally, some sleep.

Anyone who is on this sort of tour for a longer period of time loses all sense of a normal rhythm of life. Sleeping & eating is done when and where the opportunity arises: on the bus, on the plane, in the hall, it doesn't matter. Who knows when there'll be something to eat again? When we will be able to sleep again?

Everyone is tired, the crew even more so. The drivers anyway.

"The American Hotel," the once glorious hotel with its beautiful Art Nouveau cafe/restaurant, is increasingly dreadful; almost every time I'm in Amsterdam, it has changed hands, adopted a new concept, and become a notch worse again. So too this time. It's added a second, horribly noisy, tiny bar (trademark celebrity photos on the walls), even worse food in the restaurant, and a lay-man bartender (I actually have to explain to him what & how much of this or that goes into a martini).

"The American Hotel" is the standard flophouse for touring musicians. I always thought Chet Baker fell out of a window here on Friday May 13, 1988, but it was the "Prins Hendrik Hotel," not too far from here and a bit easier. 2nd floor, still dead.

Email to Karin Spaink:

Would you like to have lunch with me the day of the show?

Give me a call...

Karin Spaink is a Dutch author, feminist, anti-Scientology activist. She has multiple sclerosis.

Es tanzt das Zet-En-Es
> The C-N-S dances the

Tanzt das Zet-En-Es
> C-N-S dances the C-N-S

Das Zet-En-Es tanzt
> dances the C-N-S...

Sag Auf Wiedersehn
> Say Auf Wiedersehn

Sag Auf Wiedersehn
> Say Auf Wiedersehn

Sag Auf Wiedersehn
 Say Auf Wiedersehn
Zum Nervensystem
 To the nervous system!

From: karin spaink
Subject: Re: lunch with blixa
Date: 20. May 2008 09:19:20 GMT +1:00
To: Blixa Bargeld

The phone is not answering, I tried sms'ing you. Yes, I'd love to. I can pick you up from your hotel. Tell me when & where…

Karin drives a small, red disabled vehicle, so small that tourists photograph it; it fits between the ubiquitous conical lane dividers decorated with the three Amsterdam crosses, it is allowed to be driven on a sidewalk, it is allowed to be driven on bike paths, and it is even allowed to be driven on a highway. And: it's a two-seater. Karin picks me up in the lobby: only a crutch; the MS is better, but she's now got cancer.

Es tanzt das Zet-En-Es
Tanzt das Zet-En-Es tanzt
Das Zet-En-Es tanzt

"Yamazoto." One of the better Japanese restaurants in Europe.

Kaiseki menu, sake. Real sake. Hakushika Junmai Ginjo, served cold.

We talk about gardens, Michael Pollan's reflections from the point of view of four plants: Apples, Tulips, Marijuana, and Potatoes (Michael Pollan: *The Botany of Desire*), Arab singers (Fairuz, Abed Azrie), Samuel Butler's otherworldly utopia *Erewhon*, cancer & politics.

Sake, lots of sake.

Karin drops me off at the hotel, the midday rush must be slept off.

"De Melkweg" has been renovated, expanded.

We play in the new Milchstrasse, the old one was definitely not my favorite venue in Amsterdam, too many columns obstructing the view:

> Die Wellen
> Nagorny Karabach
> Dead Friends
> Let's Do it a Da Da
> Weil Weil Weil
> Unvollständigkeit
> Tagelang Weiss
> Rampe / Von wegen
> Die Befindlichkeit des Landes
> Sabrina
> Susej
> Ich warte

Amsterdam → Brussels. 212 km, in Benelux nothing's very far away.

Arrival for lunch. Unfortunately, I've forgotten the name of the restaurant owned by the former head of our former record company here. It was also a bit out of town; I probably wouldn't make it there in time for lunch. I just make it to "Re Source," a "Slow Food Restaurant": 10 to 2. After checking the time, the majority of the kitchen accepts the fact that my cell phone is indeed displaying the correct time, and the waitress allows me to take a seat.

> LUNCH € 25
> *Degustations du chef: entrée, plat, & dessert*

Good.

Brussels is astonishingly ugly, as if all the architectural and urban planning blunders & mistakes of the last hundred years had been collected and assembled here. Not everywhere, of course. But it is noticeable. Nevertheless: I like Belgium. For a while I spent a lot of time here. We produced almost an entire album, *Ende Neu*, in a recording studio the size of a tennis court — you could drive right in with your car, which is very helpful for recording running sixteen-stroke engines. It was located in a former hat factory in Waimes in one of the two German-speaking provinces of East Belgium. We christened it. "Stella Maris" was written there.

Unfortunately, I don't have time to visit my friend James Ensor at the Musée des Beaux Arts. Ancienne Belgique, as always, one of the best mid-sized venues in Europe:

> Die Wellen
> Nagorny Karabach

Dead Friends
Let's Do it a Da Da
Weil Weil Weil
Unvollständigkeit
Tagelang Weiss
Rampe / Von wegen
Die Befindlichkeit des Landes
Sabrina
Susej
Ich warte

Eurostar
Please check in 20 minutes before departure
22.05 11:59 BRUXELLES MI – LONDON ST-PA 22.05
13:03 KL. 1
ZUG 9127 CARRIAGE II SEAT 51 WINDOW
Solo
Non-smoker

The tunnel. Near the entrance on the French side,
in Sangrette, until recently the French Red Cross had
set up a migrant camp, the starting point for countless
attempts to reach the British Isles through the tunnel
(!). Police officers lived in the vacation settlements in
the area all year round.

The entrance is secured like a fortress.

Electric fences, barbed wire.

Flying is one thing, the tunnel another, under the
channel it's perhaps even more worrying than above
the clouds.

My case of tour flu is by now well-established. Since a legendary tour of America in the mid-'80s, when we flew the distances from city to city, my sinuses — I have none —, ears etc., have never really recovered. Flying with a cold until the eardrums almost burst during descent, the next day the same again & again & again, each time a little worse.

Sniffles → fever → inner ear infection.

Instead of the band routine of "airport — junkyard — sound check"… for me that meant: "airport — hospital — concert." By the end of the tour, a bag full of medication. From then on, flying with a cold meant: Out. Antibiotics. Gone. Once a door is kicked in, it's much easier to kick it in the next time. Here in the tunnel, too, the same effect: mucus. The eustachian tube is blocked. Lack of pressure equilibrium. Ouch. Good morning, this is going to be fun.

Trains don't fly, no descent, no landing, back above ground, things improve.

Michael Pollan: *The Omnivore's Dilemma*

I have arranged to have lunch with Sophie de Stempel & Sir Ian Holm. Sophie is a painter, former model for Lucien Freud, Ian is an actor. He was a star in the Royal Shakespeare Company in the 1960s. He played "Ash," the android, in Ridley Scott's *Alien* or more recently "Bilbo" in *Lord of the Rings*.

Originally, I wanted to invite them both to Heston Blumenthal's "The Fat Duck," but didn't get a table.

So: "Locanda Locatelli," supposedly the best Italian in London. Obscene prices. Linguini with truffle: 40 £.

Andrew Lloyd Webber is sitting behind us. Sure sure, that's London.

A lunch on the subject of illness: Parkinson's, cancer, etc.

My hotel is in Notting Hill Gate, next to a traffic circle adorned in the middle by a huge syringe sculpture filled with greenish liquid. The hotel is also an ugly monstrosity that I already know. I could tell a joke: I'm going to hit the sack, but the train has already done that, and the air-conditioning does the rest. The two pillows in the hotel bed are the disguised phone books of London, A–K & L–Z, size and hardness are consistent.

The Forum, 9–17 Highgate Road, not far from the famous Highgate Cemetery. Karl Marx: If I had time, I'd stop by again. No spray-painted arrows on the other gravestones point the way, as is the case with Jim Morrison's grave in Paris.

I have no time. From the hotel to the venue in the minibus through congested streets takes almost 2 hours again anyway. The same people who organized our concert a year ago and before are still there now. The same garbage that was outside the window of our dressing room on the terrace a year ago, three years ago, is still there. Possibly the same audience is also coming.

We played a lot in London when there was still a functioning music industry, a hip press, and we were all the rage.

We played in a hall in the summer and had the
heat turned up to watch the audience sweat.

We were on the cover of the *New Musical Express*.

We tore up the Institute of Contemporary Art.

We were on the front page of the *Daily Mail*.

(A performance re-enacted with actors at the ICA
in 2007).

We had a terrible record label.

We got "Showaddywaddy" to open for us.

We played in the Forum. We play in the Forum:

> Die Wellen
>
> Nagorny Karabach
>
> Dead Friends
>
> Let's Do it a Da Da
>
> Weil Weil Weil
>
> Unvollständigkeit
>
> Tagelang Weiss
>
> Rampe / Von wegen
>
> Die Befindlichkeit des Landes
>
> Sabrina
>
> Susej
>
> Ich warte

On the tables in the hotel bar are small laminated
cardboard signs with a "shooter selection."

> Mud Slide
>
> Screaming Blue Messiah
>
> Earthquake
>
> Peppermint Crisp
>
> Woo-Woo

Battered, Bruised & Bleeding
Brain Hemorrhage
Alabama Slammer
Slippery Nipple
B 52
Bazooka Joe
Bubble Gum

England has a "binge-drinking" problem.

From the elevator to my room door, it's a hundred of my steps, pretty much. When I arrived this afternoon, I had to go up & down several times, first because the key didn't work, then because the room hadn't been cleaned at all, and then again to buy a bottle of water.

The first few times I spent counting the steps each time, just from one to a hundred.

Then I started to divide the way into bars, up to my room door there are twenty-five four-four bars.

Divided into bars, the corridor starts to get more interesting, the regularity of the doors, the art prints, the fire doors: rhythms.

It's about twenty-six or twenty-seven three-quarter measures when my wife calls, I got a little off counting. It's afternoon in San Francisco.

It's eight hours later in London.

The maid has annoyingly disposed of my bottle of water. You can't drink tap water here, so I'll stick to the wine, but that doesn't want to be drunk either. Room service or masturbation? Nothing really offers any perspectives. A strange state, underlaid with the

unforgiving processing noise of my hearing problem,
which is then the last thing, after the TV noises, the
voices coming from the books. After all that has been
done away with, it creeps away, like an afterimage,
into an afterthought, into my half-asleep head, thinking about Hartmut, my bookseller, the internet, the
loss of my last mobile phone. By morning, this has
evolved into a conference with my bookseller, my assistant, & others; condensed into a not-even spurious
concentrate: a a strategy intended to assist my bookseller in penetrating the internet, a leap, a growing
niche that could be conquered with a hangman's mask,
orienting itself on the very roof of the world.
— Something like that.

    Elevator
    Taxi
    London Heathrow Airport
    Baggage cart

        BARGELD/B MR
        BA/GOLD 74125115
        FROM LONDON LHR
        TO BERLIN TXL
        BA 986 23 MAY 16 05

    British Airways Lounge: The food is inedible, I
know from experience, so better not order anything.
    "Kettle Chips" & champagne.
    FAZ/SZ: Lounge-reading.

Eight out of ten guests are men, balancing laptops on their knees, phone or Blackberry in hand. Because they've traveled so much, they all have a gold card & are allowed in here. I travel a lot, too.

I have a gold card, too.

Escalator

Escalator

Moving sidewalk

Airplane

On approach, grimacing, open-mouthed, I try to press my ears open, to ease the pain. The couple in my row, center & window seat, looking out, think the Havel and adjacent Berlin waterways are the Mecklenburg Lake District, and that the former American listening station on Teufelsberg is the new Reichstag. The Trümmerberg is the new government district. Great idea. Berlin is so flat, we just heap up little hills everywhere, called mountains (Berge) in Berlin vernacular, on which important buildings are then erected. The Stadtschloss could also be rebuilt in this way: simply cart the original rubble together, heap it up to form a mountain of rubble, cover it with topsoil & put something important on top of it: the Ministry of Culture, state ministries, something like that.

Berlin Tegel Airport

Baggage cart

Taxi

Elevator

My ears are fucked again.

Dinner at the "Grill Royal" with Carl-Johan Vallgren, a Swedish writer, Mote Sinabel, our Japanese
designer, and my assistant Andrea Schmid:

If Strindberg, the misogynist sociopath, had been here, he
would have immediately spread about the noble art of fanta-
sizing about the cunt, which is not particularly original when
you have a dozen Fine de Claire oysters on a bed of ice in front
of you, after all, that creates certain associations, especially in
company with his late incarnation, the Swedish writer Vallgren.
The Café Royal was around the corner, Unter den Linden 33,
where E.T.A. Hoffmann and Heine used to drink each other
under the table, and of course Hartmut has to show up, the old
bookworm with his fondness for insane Scandinavian artists,
and pontificate about his idea to bring the classic artists' pub
Zum Schwarzen Ferkel back to life for a weekend. Vallgren may
get the honorable assignment of appearing as Strindberg, al-
though something tells me he'd be better off as the dour Munch,
or possibly the corny Przybyszewski, if that role isn't assigned
to me, who was, after all, despite everything, not only the guy
who kidnapped Munch's muse Dagny Juel, but also a de facto
genius composer. My Japanese photographer guest of honor at
the table doesn't quite seem to get a handle on this kind of sub-
tle Berliniana; but who fuckin' cares about dead poets? Well,
I do! Heiner Müller once advised me to read Jean Paul, & for
that I am eternally grateful. Jean Paul is God, if anyone were
to ask me, and the Swede in front of me unexpectedly agrees.
Nice little vintage, by the way, this Saxon Auslese they serve
here with the fish. And the waiter looks like he's escaped

*from a Fassbinder film, his head grotesquely large, just like the monster in Vallgren's novel, which, to my shame, I haven't read; a drop of sweat has taken up residence on his left temple, which is what happens when it's 25 degrees at 11:00 on a May evening.**

Back to my apartment at Reichsstrasse 1, always wide enough for two tanks, from Warsaw to Paris.

I doze a bit on the couch, one hand on the buttons, the other around a glass of wine, stupor to the point of sleep. Here's to tomorrow.

My office has arranged an appointment with my ENT doctor: the usual program, the usual diagnosis: sinusitis, inner ear infection on the left, middle, and inner ear infection on the right.

The usual medications: Antibiotics, Voltaren, nose drops. If I flew again, it would get even worse and my chance of being able to take the return flight to San Francisco afterwards would be considerably reduced. So Athens, the last concert of this tour, is probably cancelled. Too bad: I ♥ Athens.

In our career spanning three decades, we have only cancelled three concerts:

1993 Élysée Montmartre/Paris because of volume problems.

1993 Trocadero/Philadelphia, Pennsylvania due to lack of PA.

And now: Fuzz/Athens because of my inability to fly.

When the Allies divided the city of Berlin into sectors after WWII, each got an airport: The Soviets got Schönefeld Airport, the English got Datow Airfield, the French got the former airship airfield in Reinickendorf, which was used in the meantime as the Tegel rocket firing range & then as a military training area. During the airlift, they established a fourth Berlin airport. The Americans used Tempelhof Airport. Up to and including Ronald Reagan, the planes of American presidents landed there during state visits. Columbiahalle, a former sports hall for the American troops stationed in Berlin, is directly opposite Tempelhof Airport. We have played here several times:

> Die Wellen
> Nagorny Karabach
> Dead Friends
> Let's Do it a Da Da
> Weil Weil Weil
> Unvollständigkeit
> Tagelang Weiss
> Rampe / Von wegen
> Die Befindlichkeit des Landes
> Sabrina
> Susej
> Ich warte

Aftershow party.
End of tour.
European Roundup: What's missing?
Zürich, Venice ...

Reykjavik: "What problems do you have here?" "Junkies and suicides in the winter..."

Madrid, Manchester, Rennes in Bretagne ...

Rotterdam: Under a hail of projectiles, took the stage as the opening act for U2.

Florence, Bratislava, Arhus, Antwerp...

Klagenfurt: Arrested for imitating a cab radio...

Malaga, Krems, Nantes, Reggio Emilia.

Bolzano: Our instruments had to be carried up the mountain...

Potsdam, Ljubljana, Ghent, Leeds...

Turin: With the band bus on the roof test track of the futuristic former Fiat factory...

Thessaloniki, Belgrade, Glasgow, Strasbourg...

Dublin: No, I didn't kick in the glass door, look at the video camera footage... I didn't kick it in.

Istanbul, Salzburg, Venice, Krakow...

Rome: I dreamt of my death, purgatory, and thereafter...

Don't misunderstand me:

I ♥ Europe.

* The italicized passages were written — at my request and *as if from my perspective* — by:

1. Bruno Pisek (p. 29–31)
2. Rocko Schamoni (pp. 83–84)
3. Carl-Johann Vallgren (pp. 102–103)

AFTERWORD

A loop, without a beginning or end[1]

When I first came across Blixa Bargeld's book EUROPA KREUZWEISE: EINE LITANEI, it was the subtitle, first of all, that caught my attention. Having grown up with a brand of "fuck up — go to mass — get drunk — fuck up again — go to confession — rinse, repeat" Midwest (southern Illinois) Catholicism myself (which I eventually escaped to become "just" a professional fuck-up and drunk, minus the religion), I was more than familiar with what a litany is. In fact, once I had read the book, it may have been part of the reason that a potential translation was initially intriguing to me. I love the occasional absurdity of lists, and also mind-numbing repetition (whether in a religious context or not), which can leave one stupefied, perhaps coming across as bizarre, cultish, or even humorous, for within the repetition & the recurring incantations is an inherent sort of strangeness that can only induce one to embark on a simultaneous mental (and parallel) journey. And if that litany, as it is in this case, is composed of playlists, badly written hotel descriptions, & quirky restaurant menus, underpinned by the inherent absurdity of the rock 'n' roll

1. Blixa Bargeld, on April 13, 2022, from an interview conducted by the translator for this Afterword.

lifestyle, of the tours, of the soundchecks, and of the routines... (repetitions of whatever sort)... then you have a recipe for a unique book, to say the least.

At first glance this particular book appeared as if it might be a tour diary, or a recounting of life with Einstürzende Neubauten on the road... but a few pages in I recognized that this it most certainly *is not*. It is rather a semi-fictional account that reads in some ways like an ongoing text that is constantly turning circles upon itself. And it purports to relate events *&* things seen and experienced, anchored by a structure, a framework, designed from setlists and restaurant menus. Yet the further one reads one realizes that, much like an eyewitness at an accident or some other slightly peculiar event one experiences, the recollection (or the depiction) reported by the individual who experienced the events depicted herein is somewhat colored by what they might have seen ... or didn't see at all ... or perhaps in fact did, but at some other time *&* place entirely.

In this particular case, that someone is Blixa Bargeld, who in 2008 was approached by the Austrian publisher Residenz Verlag to write a book for their "litany" series. Residenz intended to publish a whole series of litanies written by different writers, artists, and musicians, all of similar length, and they wanted to know if he might like to give it a try. (They eventually published three, this being the second). The idea fascinated him, but before actually embarking on the project, Bargeld asked a friend, Dr. Maria Zinfert, for her literary viewpoint about just what a litany is.[2] Dr. Zinfert offered three key points: 1) a litany is an oral form that is intended to be spoken aloud; 2) it is basically never-ending, thriving on repetition within the same structure; and 3) it is typically rooted in a liturgical context.

Upon consideration, Blixa told Claudia Romeder, his editor at Residenz, that the project would interest him, deciding to take the form of the litany as a model to develop a structure for the text, using the upcoming Einstürzende Neubauten tour of Europe as the material out of which to create his book. *"I didn't set out to write a tour diary, but rather told the publisher: 'I'll leave out the middle bit. I don't want to talk about concerts, and I don't want to talk about music. Instead I'll take the movement of the tour through Europe as the focal point of the text."*[3]

2. Dr. Zinfert had been the editorial supervisor for Blixa Bargeld and Kain Karawahn's *"Headcleaner," 233° Celsius* (1999). She also had a hand in *Serialbathroomdummyrun*, which was published by Hartmut Fischer's infamous Berlin-based *Juliettes Literatursalon* in 1997.

3. Following the publication of the book, and in an interview with Thomas Wagner of *Junge Welt* in early 2009, Bargeld noted that the "Duden Dictionary of Foreign Words" states: Litany: 1. a prayer of intercession sung in turn; 2. monotonous speech, whereby I rather fall into the last category. "Ich sollte der West-Hamlet werden," interview with Blixa Bargeld in *Junge Welt* (02/21/2009).

Taking the definition of the word into account, two things specifically interested him about it.[4] A litany is in fact not a literary genre, or specific form, but rather a religious (specifically, Catholic) one that a) is potentially endless, has no "high point" and also no beginning or end, but just runs in a loop, and b) generally, it is a text that is spoken, a verbal text. In approaching the book, it soon became clear that the "Alles Wieder Offen" European Tour in 2008 would be the perfect backbone to the book after all. And as he'd already been in nearly all the scheduled cities before, this too was going to be a repetition in the sense of a litany, namely, the same thing again & again, with the potential that this particular version of it could prove endlessly and especially appealing.

A further aspect that interested him: At the time of writing the book, Bargeld & his wife were splitting time between three different cities at once, namely San Francisco and Beijing, with Berlin in the middle.

4. Litany: In the liturgy of the Catholic Church, the alternating prayer between the prayer leader and the congregation responding with unchanging supplications, a rendered 'long-winded, monotonous enumeration, repeatedly recited lament, exhortation.' → letanīe, early German letaney, litanie, litaney are borrowed from Late Latin litanīa, also letanīa, lætanīa 'supplication procession, supplication formulas recited alternately in processions and at mass.' → Late Latin litanīa, in turn, is borrowed from Greek litanēia (λιτανεία) 'petition, supplication'; to Greek litanēuein (λιτανεύειν) 'ask, plead.' The development of the present form of prayer began in the early Middle Ages.

In a sense he was already criss-crossing the world; the European tour would add another component to that mix. "*I knew that for work with Neubauten, I would always need to be in Berlin. And then I would go from Berlin either to Beijing and from Beijing, I would fly to San Francisco, and from San Francisco back to Berlin. And that was my life ... well, until we gave up. Eventually we decided, for various reasons, to give up San Francisco and make it only Berlin.*" [5] In light of this, obviously there was a bit of irony in the title: "CROSSwise."

In talking about the book after it was published, Bargeld wanted to emphasize one thing especially, & if anything should be reiterated, it is that the book is semi-fictional, it is literature, it is "put together": partly true, partly not, and that the sequence as it is written never actually happened as it occurs in this book. Before embarking on the tour, Bargeld had already known what was awaiting him: sitting in a bus, checking into a hotel, soundchecks, concerts, the bus again, etc., etc., etc. The repetition of the same structure, schema, again and again and again: *a litany.* And again, importantly, the potential that this is also endless in nature, with no "high point," or "development" — and so the book functions as a loop, created with the hope that after reading the last sentence, you could theoretically turn straight back to page one & just keep reading again, an endlessly revolving door. Oh wait, we've said that already, haven't we ...

5. Interview with the translator, April 13, 2022.

Taken a step further and broken down to its bare essence, the book could simply be refined to a bunch of lists, of repetitive incantations, the responses, and the incantations again. And so on. This is what the book ultimately achieves in conveying, much like what Dadaist Walter Serner might have said but in another context, fully confronting *die Langeweile* (boredom). The setlists, while not 100% exactly precisely repetitive, are in and of themselves *repetitive elements* of the cycle. And these almost invariably end with the song "Ich Warte" (I'm Waiting), the conclusion of every setlist in every city... which is duly taken up again at the next venue and begins again with "Die Wellen" (The Waves). If one reads the text and setlists aloud one can see that, although not intentionally so, there is a monotonous rhythm, and this is where the oral aspect of the litany works as a kind of incantation.

For Bargeld, ultimately, what of the book is true and what fiction, this didn't matter much. What was important to understand was that it was not just about a Neubauten tour and not just *about* Europe, but the experience *of* Europe in this revolving tour-machine. These days, the songs filling the setlists also certainly conjure up particular images for the reader, especially in light of the horrors being experienced on the easternmost edges of Europe in savage war. Who cannot read the song titles without immediately hearing the driving rhythms behind *Nagorny Karabach*, *Weil Weil Weil*, or *Die Befindlichkeit des Landes*, etc.? Indeed, if the reader

takes the setlist as a soundtrack to listen to the book
while reading, the feeling is enhanced even further.

In a way, of course, as noted, the book touches on
all the typical aspects of a tour, and it has a lot to do
with it, but as noted, focusing on the tour was not the
original intention. For although this is a book about a
Neubauten tour, the band itself remains on the fringes
in the actual text. It is as if (to paraphrase Hamlet, or
as Bargeld might say, the "West-Hamlet") "the setlist
is the thing / wherein we catch the conscience of the
king." As in any liturgy or procession, there is the top
level, the things that are being said and done (the actual incantations, here: the setlists, the trips, the hotels,
the restaurants) and then the subtext, those things we
might experience "running in the background," the
specifics, if you will (the menus, the details about the
cities, the recall). The concerts themselves are, in a
sense, an afterthought. *Ein Loop ohne Ende und Anfang.*
So this is not a tour diary at all, but a text in which the
writer takes the freedom to invent things and combine
things from completely different places and even from
different *years...* and so when talking about Prague,
or Klagenfurt, or wherever, this could also have even
happened with Nick Cave or Neubauten... everything
is a blur. But the experiences, either actual or "half-
remembered," they are most definitely real.

When EUROPA was first published it was generally well-received, albeit with a qualifier, or some
version of: The man who was once a house squatter

in collapsing buildings has now become a gourmand frequenting the finest of restaurants and is especially interested in the menus. Looking back on the book over 10 years later, Bargeld commented, "*The setlist itself is a menu. And if I then talk about a, well, not a menu, but a menu in the sense of, an order of different courses, then: right, we're very close to a setlist.*"[6] However, many reviewers (and fans) were still pining for the *Tanz Debil*, *Halber Mensch*, *ZNS*, and *Zerstörte Zelle* mayhem of their early years, not a recommendation for a good restaurant or insight on good shoe stores in Milan. But anyone who had followed the trajectory of the band and can follow the evolution thereof in subsequent years (especially from 1995 onward) knows the material had gradually become more refined, linear, and clean. Poetic, even. However, that sense of (literary) refinement was always there, even in the late 1980s and early 1990s, a little later after a period when they had been setting stages on fire and getting thrown out of town. And, after all, it was Neubauten that worked directly with Heiner Müller on *Hamletmaschine*[7] and Werner Schwab on *Faustmusik: Mein Brustkorb, mein Helm*,"[8] both of which

6. Interview with the translator, April 13, 2022.
7. *Hamletmachine*, including music by Einstürzende Neubauten, was released as an album and CD in 1990–91. Bargeld played the part of Prince Hamlet & Gudrun Gut played Ophelia.
8. Werner Schwab (1958–1994) was an Austrian writer and dramatist. Schwab, a heavy drinker who wrote searing plays, was the author of *Faust — Mein Brustkorb: Mein Helm*,

any fan cherishes as seminal moments in the band's history. So, by 2009, people might have anticipated — & perhaps shouldn't have been surprised by — what could be coming in a Blixa Bargeld book.

With respect to culinary matters, as Bargeld might have said when he was writing the book (and definitely says today): *Life is too short to eat bad food.* And anyone who has become familiar with him in interviews throughout the years, or personally knows him, is aware that food itself plays an important role in his daily routines. Again, in this instance, this is certainly why the menus (also recurring and repetitive in their humorously odd way) also form a part of the backbone of the book. Regarding the dining-related aspect of the book, shortly after it was published, Bargeld stated:

> *I just have the talent to position myself between two worlds. If you decide to leave out the concerts (on the one hand), of course you're left with hotels, restaurants, and a few museums (on the other). But when I quote a menu in the book, I'm not primarily concerned with what there is to eat, but with the language. After all,*

performed (and recorded) with Thomas Thieme as Faust, Blixa Bargeld as Mephisto, Günter Rüger as Busho, Gabriele Völsch as Margarethen, and music by Einstürzende Neubauten. It was recorded at the Hans-Otto-Theater in Potsdam between October 1994 and June 1995 by Boris Wilsdorf & Thomas Stern and released as a CD in 1996. Schwab's body was found lifeless on New Year's Day 1994. His output in his short life is regarded as exceptional.

*the first menu reads like a joke: there you are, sitting in
a three-star restaurant in Germany, drowning in a French-
German babble of language. About 50 percent of what's
in the book never happened (that way) anyway. And I
knew from the beginning what the last sentence would
be ("I love Europe"). It's only when I come back to Europe
that I truly realize that. All the places I mention in my
book are somehow embedded in my nervous system.* [9]

Interesting that Bargeld here invokes his "nervous
system" — again circling back round to 1985 and *ZNS*
(*CNS, Central Nervous System*):

> *The Ce-En-Es / dances the Ce-En-Es dances /
> the Ce-En-Es / dances / the Ce-En-Es / it circulates /
> circulation / it's all running in circles /
> all along the wall / swings & roundabouts.*

So, having repeated ourselves (a bit) as well in
relating exactly what this whole litany business was
about and what Bargeld sought to achieve, we could
fancy him saying, much like the famous quote in
Lynch's *Lost Highway*: "I like to remember things my

---

9. „Hausbesetzer sind konservativ": Blixa Bargeld im Interview mit profil. Blixa Bargeld über Punks, Heroin und
Speisekarten. ("Squatters are Conservative": Blixa Bargeld in an interview with *Profil Magazine*. Blixa Bargeld on
Punks, Heroin, and Menus.) Interview with Karin Cerny
(03/07/2009).

own way. How *I remembered them*, not necessarily *the way they happened*," albeit with his own slight variation — "… or … how I *imagined* they might have happened." Ultimately, we are left with a unique love letter to Europe, forming a gracious loop, without beginning or end.

Mark Kanak
May 2022
Berlin

COLOPHON

EUROPE CROSSWISE: A LITANY
was handset in InDesign CC.

The text font is *Swift*.
The display font is PP *Gosha Sans*.

Book design & typesetting: Alessandro Segalini
Cover design: Alessandro Segalini & CMP

EUROPE CROSSWISE: A LITANY
is published by Contra Mundum Press.

Contra Mundum Press   New York · London · Melbourne

CONTRA MUNDUM PRESS

Dedicated to the value & the indispensable importance of the individual voice, to works that test the boundaries of thought & experience.

The primary aim of Contra Mundum is to publish translations of writers who in their use of form and style are *à rebours*, or who deviate significantly from more programmatic & spurious forms of experimentation. Such writing attests to the volatile nature of modernism. Our preference is for works that have not yet been translated into English, are out of print, or are poorly translated, for writers whose thinking & æsthetics are in opposition to timely or mainstream currents of thought, value systems, or moralities. We also reprint obscure and out-of-print works we consider significant but which have been forgotten, neglected, or overshadowed.

There are many works of fundamental significance to *Weltliteratur* (& *Weltkultur*) that still remain in relative oblivion, works that alter and disrupt standard circuits of thought — these warrant being encountered by the world at large. It is our aim to render them more visible.

For the complete list of forthcoming publications, please visit our website. To be added to our mailing list, send your name and email address to: info@contramundum.net

Contra Mundum Press
P.O. Box 1326
New York, NY 10276
USA

OTHER CONTRA MUNDUM PRESS TITLES

SOME FORTHCOMING TITLES

THE FUTURE OF KULCHUR
A PATRONAGE PROJECT

LEND CONTRA MUNDUM PRESS (CMP) YOUR SUPPORT

With bookstores and presses around the world struggling to survive, and many actually closing, we are forming this patronage project as a means for establishing a continuous & stable foundation to safeguard our longevity. Through this patronage project we would be able to remain free of having to rely upon government support &/or other official funding bodies, not to speak of their timelines & impositions. It would also free CMP from suffering the vagaries of the publishing industry, as well as the risk of submitting to commercial pressures in order to persist, thereby potentially compromising the integrity of our catalog.

CAN YOU SACRIFICE $10 A WEEK FOR KULCHUR?

For the equivalent of merely 2–3 coffees a week, you can help sustain CMP and contribute to the future of kulchur. To participate in our patronage program we are asking individuals to donate $500 per year, which amounts to $42/month, or $10/week. Larger donations are of course welcome and beneficial. All donations are tax-deductible through our fiscal sponsor Fractured Atlas. If preferred, donations can be made in two installments. We are seeking a minimum of 300 patrons per year and would like for them to commit to giving the above amount for a period of three years.

Part tax-deductible donation, part exchange, for your contribution you will receive every CMP book published during the patronage period as well as 20 books from our back catalog. When possible, signed or limited editions of books will be offered as well.

Your contribution will help with basic general operating expenses, yearly production expenses (book printing, warehouse & catalog fees, etc.), advertising and outreach, and editorial, proofreading, translation, typography, design and copyright fees. Funds may also be used for participating in book fairs and staging events. Additionally, we hope to rebuild the *Hyperion* section of the website in order to modernize it.

From Pericles to Mæcenas & the Renaissance patrons, it is the magnanimity of such individuals that have helped the arts to flourish. Be a part of helping your kulchur flourish; be a part of history.

To lend your support & become a patron, please visit the subscription page of our website: contramundum.net/subscription

For any questions, write us at: info@contramundum.net

Lightning Source UK Ltd.
Milton Keynes UK
UKHW011828220922
409294UK00001B/60